DEAR ANDREW

Robert M. Goor

Goor, Robert M.: Dear Andrew

ISBN-13: 978-1533350268

ISBN-10: 1533350264

1. Death, Grief, Bereavement—Memoir, 2. Letters to Son—Memoir. 3. Loss of Son—Memoir. 4. Loss of Son—Memoir. 5. Father Grief—Memoir. 6. Peace after Loss—Memoir. 7. Healing after Loss—Memoir.

www.dearandrew.net

Dedication

This book is dedicated to Leah, Andrew and Hannah, and to children of all ages everywhere.

December 17, 2001

Dear Reader,

It seems perfectly natural, doesn't it? If you have a question, go look it up in a book. I've been doing it all my life. I was taught to do it in school, and now it's my first instinct. If I need a fact, I find a book with the answer. But, what if the question is not one of fact? What if the question is about the meaning of life, for example?

Well, some time ago, I found myself browsing aimlessly in a bookstore when it suddenly occurred to me that I wasn't so aimless. To the contrary, I was looking purposefully for answers. I could feel it; but, answers to what? I was dissatisfied, out of harmony with myself and with the world, and I wanted answers. Then, I knew. I could not find answers until I knew what my questions were, and there were no books in the store that could help with that. Where, then? Somehow, I knew that I had to pursue my quest within, and I left the store without a purchase.

That was when the idea seriously crossed my mind that I had to finish these letters. And so it seems ironic that I now commit to a book the telling of the most painful quest of my life. Perhaps the reading of this book will help someone else with his or her questions and answers as the writing has helped me with mine.

On May 19, 1988, I watched helplessly as my son, Andrew, was hit by a truck and killed. He was eight years and eight months old, almost to the hour. And so I wrote. And so I write. I wrote to him because I had to find a way to stay close, to continue to relate to him, and to find myself again. And I wrote to share my letters, so as not to feel so alone after what I have learned has been the most

1

isolating experience of my life. Hence the name of the book. I would not, for the world, wish that anyone live where I live, and have lived, but I do accept and cherish visitors.

Grief and loss are inextricably bound up with fundamental life questions, so no grief is simple. My grief over Andrew's death has been made even more complex by the turmoil of his last years of life and the violence of his death. A part of my process has been the telling of what happened, as I have become ready to tell it, and to know it myself.

At times, it has been healing for me to share my letters by reading them aloud. Somehow, that helps to "mail" them, and therefore, many of the letters were written with that form of "oral postage" in mind. Perhaps that is the way they are meant to be experienced.

I have learned, both from my own experience and from that of other bereaved parents, that grief is not well understood, nor well tolerated, in our society. Grief is an inherently isolating state. The sense of loss and dislocation contribute to a general lack of connection with oneself, and with the universe as a whole. This is true of all losses, but losing a child causes the most intense grief. Such depth of feeling is not easily shared.

Fortunately, however, I have been blessed with friends and family who have been incredibly supportive, and without whom I could not have reached this point in my life. These amazing people have even gone so far as to thank me for sharing my grief with them.

I especially want to thank: my wonderful wife, Linda, who encourages my continued relationship with Andrew, and whose love, patience and insights have sustained me and helped me heal during our whole time together; my grief counselor, Anne Carey, whose encouragement and gentle but persistent pushing helped keep me moving in the early years of my grief work; my therapists, Roz and Fred Lessing, who, with kindness and wisdom, have been my guides in the deepest sense, from the beginning; my therapist, Jennifer Cantrell, who, with patience, understanding and reassurance, has helped me to heal the traumas in my life; and all my friends, who have been supportive and who continue to include Andrew in our lives together. All of these people, and others, have shared my nightmare, and I have learned that I can survive almost anything if I am not alone—and that emotional isolation is worse than death. Thank you all, for helping me to find myself, and my words.

Now that I am done, I am sad—sad for what I have written, sad for what I have thought, and sad for what has eluded me. I am sad for what Andrew never got to have, and what we never got to have.

This letter to you, dear reader, which appears first, was written last. The rest of the letters are to Andrew, with love.

Yours,
Rob Goor

May 25, 1988

Dear Andrew,

I have hardly been alone since it happened, and I still can't talk about it. Sometimes, I think that the whole world has gone crazy, and I can't believe anything that has happened. Maybe I'm the one going crazy. The world seems to be going off on one path and I've angled off sharply on another. Or maybe I'm just completely stopped. I don't know. I just know that I feel knocked out of orbit, careening out of control, and lost.

My friends have stayed close to my side. Now, even when I have been alone, I know how to reach them quickly, but I also know that they will need to get on with their lives. What will I do then? For me, there will be no getting on. In fact, I awake each morning to hear the traffic from Woodward Avenue, and my first reaction is anger that the world could go on casually without you, as if nothing had happened.

Sometimes, being alone is a relief. I am spared the mirror of my grief in the faces of my friends. Usually, however, being alone is intolerable, as my mind runs wild in a field of tangled and tortured memories. Often, I feel you near me. Incredibly, I have even seen you near me, and, in tears, you have asked me, "What happened?" I shake my head to drive away what I surely cannot be seeing, but you return. I don't know what to think, and especially what to do. Surely, all of this is impossible. Doesn't it mean that I'm crazy if I experience the impossible? How can I share this? Who would believe me?

Worst of all has been my fear that you would come to me in the night, at the threshold of sleep, and that you would appear as you did after the accident. Did I say fear?

No, I know how to describe fear, but this is terror, of a depth that I can't begin to convey. Even in the midst of my worst nightmares, however frightening they may have been, I have always had the sense, deep down, that they are only dreams after all. They will be over when I wake. But, I know that I will never awaken from this nightmare. This dream is real, and lasts a lifetime. There is no waking. And if I must live my nightmare, what awaits me in my sleep?

Yet, I cannot describe what horror I saw, the devastation to your body, and the horrors I fear to see again. Do I hold back out of concern for you, or for others, or is it because I, myself, cannot face the full reality of what has happened? I don't know.

Knowing has been ripped from me, as has everything else that once guided my life. All that has remained is a kind of truth, and even comfort, in the intensity of shared feeling. That is my only sunlight. And so I have hardly been alone, for fear of shadow.

This one thing I know, however. My life will never again be what it was. The future, as I once knew it, is gone.

Love,
Dad

On May 26, 1988, I started to write, whether a journal entry or a letter to Andrew I will never know, because an entirely foreign letter flowed from my fingertips. It was a letter from Andrew to me, and it was signed the way he usually signed his art, with his first name spelled backwards:

Dear Dad,

I don't exactly know what has happened to me. One minute, I was riding Nate's wagon down his driveway, and the next minute, I found myself looking at me on the ground. I saw you run up to me and then I saw you run to Mom's and bang on the door. Then, you came back. I saw you cry and scream. Then, there were a lot of people I didn't know, and I saw them take me away on a stretcher. But I didn't feel any pain!

Actually, I haven't seen anything, but somehow I know, or feel what I've told you. I don't know how to describe it. I'm uncomfortable with it and I don't exactly want to talk about it, but I want to know what has happened. I'm scared. How can I "see" me on the ground? If that is my body, how can I feel separate from it? I wasn't moving, and the people covered me all up with a sheet. Does that mean I'm dead? How can that be? I don't want to be dead.

I have seen you cry a lot, and I don't want you to hurt.

Love,
Werdna

May 27, 1988

Dear Andrew,

Everything is leading me in one direction. I must tell you what happened to you, but how? The idea of telling you anything seems so crazy to me. But, then, everything that has happened is beyond comprehension. Yet, I want to believe that your spirit lingers, that you have communicated with me, and that you can feel my responses. I want to believe that your letter, as painful as it is for me to read, really is from you. As difficult as this transition will be for us both, the alternative, that everything is simply over for you, for us, seems unimaginable to me.

The mere fact that I am writing to you, and that it gives me comfort, betrays a subtle belief that I am somehow touching you. And so I will continue. I must continue. We have had a changing and growing relationship since you were born. Perhaps we will go on relating, in spite of everything. Until I am surer of myself, I will shore up my fragile faith with hope.

Otherwise, I am faced with nothing but despair. If only I knew that you were alive and safe somewhere, I could live with never seeing you again. It would be difficult, but I could do it. If only I could believe in a future for you, I could tolerate the pain of separation. But, this life, this not knowing, this wondering, is more than I can bear. And so, yes, I want to believe that I'm not crazy, and that the evidences of my senses are real. Please, help me believe!

But, what must you be feeling? What must you be going through? I can only imagine that you must be feeling frightened and totally bewildered. Most of all, I feel pain for your loss of your whole future, whether it's with or without me. I would talk to you about it, but I choke on the words. My mind seems to seize at the very concept. So, you see, I just can't face you with what I have to say.

I still can't tell anyone any details of what happened, and I am only just now beginning to be able to be alone during the day. I tried to spend a night alone, but, I experienced such terror that I could not stay home, and drove to Dale's house. Yes, I drove a short distance. It is one of the first times. I don't yet trust myself behind the wheel of a car—what if I have an accident? What if I hurt someone? I cannot bear the thought.

I don't know when or how I'll go back to work. I don't even know when or how I'll go back to life.

Love, as always,
Dad

May 29, 1988

Dear Andrew,

At last, I can be alone, and no one else is here. But, I am not alone, for you are in every room in this house. And I can't stand it anymore! I know what happened to you. I saw what happened to you. And I have to tell you what everyone else already knows.

Andrew, this hurts so much for me to write, much less to think. You were hit by a car and killed. You're dead! How can it be? I can never hold your sweet body in my arms again. I don't understand. How can it be? I can never smooth your hair and smile at you, except in my memories. How can it be? I don't understand.

And you, you must feel all sorts of things. You have lost your whole life. You have been asking me, and now I have told you. Somehow, the pain of your knowing, on top of my own grief, is more than I can bear, and I find myself curled up on the floor, the events and feelings of the last days coursing through me.

As I lie there, on the carpet, I hear a fluttering sound over my head, and, a few moments later, I seem to hear the sound of a door opening and closing. Then, there is silence. You are gone. I can no longer feel your presence. What did I hear?

I know you're upset. Who wouldn't be? But, will you be back? Now, I'm really alone. As hard as it was to tell you, though, I feel some relief that you know. Right now, I just feel an incredible ache for you. God, I miss you so! I can't imagine that you're gone, and a part of me screams out "No!" when I think of it. I can't imagine saying goodbye to you. I can't even begin to comprehend that this is so final. What am I to do?

And I feel so alone with what I saw. I relive it over and over, but I just can't tell anyone about it. I don't know why, and I don't have to know. I just know that I can't. Maybe someday I'll be able to let it out, but not now.

I'm so tired, so weary, and I ache so. I don't feel much like going on, but I do, at least for today. I love you always.

Love,
Dad

June 30, 1988

Dear Andrew,

I miss you more than I can say. I dream so much, I awake exhausted, as if I have been working all night, and some say I have. Even when you are not in my dreams, I feel that they are about you.

I had such a dream last night, about a wall. It was a perfectly straight low wall, temptingly low, yet high enough to bar my eyes. I stood several feet away, just looking at it, and aching to know what was hidden from me.

On my side of the wall, there was no shelter, nothing but a barren plain that extended forever all around me up to this endless barrier. There was a stark unreality to my surroundings, and I realized that neither the wall nor I cast a shadow—the sand underfoot had no trace of darkness.

The wall itself was an undefined composite material, so coarsely formed and so sharp that it reminded me of a giant rasp. The top of the wall was some sort of brick, with a slight overhang, though how I could tell with no shadow, I do not know, nor did I question. There was no way to tell how thick the wall was, but I sensed that it was impenetrable.

No, the only way to the other side was over the top, which was so enticingly low, and yet, surely, no living thing could climb it! I certainly had no desire to try. I was content to keep my distance.

Nevertheless, I felt that somehow everything would be different for me and all my questions would be answered, if only I could get a glimpse of the other side. At last, I would know all I need to know! So there I stood, torn between my longing to see and my need to stay, while the harsh sunlight baked my hapless plain, and me along with it.

Andrew, I know what this wall is, and it is real, not a dream. This is the wall between what is and what isn't, between my today and all our yesterdays, between the harsh light of day and the eternal light of love, between spirit and flesh, between you and me. So tenuous is this low barrier, and yet so solid.

And the wind! I almost forgot to mention the wind. It was a wind out of my past, out of the past of others before me. A ghostly voice, hot on my face, it was a rustling that seemed to emanate directly from the sand itself, telling of ruins in the desert and the death of a people. It was a desolate wind bearing the taste of sand, a bitter wind bereft of the scent of life, a relentless wind that whispered the end of time.

That is the wind I felt in the dream. I have felt it before. I feel it still.

Love,
Dad

July 6, 1988

Dear Andrew,

Today, I have so many feelings that just swirl around inside me. Sometimes, I feel as though I'm on a roller coaster, and it never stops.

First, I'm slowly climbing, inching my way higher, as I wonder, was there something I could have done or said that would have changed what happened to you? Would anything you and I talked about have worked? Questions, questions ... and no answers. Was there something that I did or said that caused all this? Could I have run and stopped the wagon? Could I have knocked you off? Did the wagon have a way to steer? Do you remember? You were holding on to the sides and couldn't have steered anyway. Why were you holding the sides of the wagon? In the last few weeks, you showed up with an unusual number of cuts and bruises on your arms and legs. Why? Were you taking a lot of risks? I had a recurring dream that I tried, over and over, to run and stop the wagon, but I couldn't get there in time. Then, I finally got there in time. What a relief! But, you were already dead. So many unanswered questions. What will I do?

Then, I reach the pinnacle, and gravity takes over, as the mad energy stored during my ascent unwinds. And I realize that I'm angry with so many people. First, there were the people who were directly and, perhaps, indirectly involved in your death. Then there were a lot of people who contributed to making your life miserable during the divorce, and leading up to the accident. I know, maybe they don't matter any more, but right now, I'm angry with anyone who caused you pain. I'm even angry with the police, who have not asked me what happened to you. But, the hardest for me is the pure and seemingly endless anger that I feel just because …

But, I have hit bottom, my rage temporarily spent, and I feel that I am winding through curves, tossed left and right, and my energy turns inward. When I think of you laughing, playing, or snuggling, I just hurt so much for you and for us. Some people have said that you're "better off". I hate that! But, how do I know if you're not? Others have said that you're doing the work you "need" to do. And how do I know you aren't? Several months before, I began to accept that you did know your own process, and that you did know what you needed. But that is so hard to accept right now. How could your being dead be what you "need", when you were so full of life, and life has so much to offer? Perhaps there are answers to this, but I certainly can't feel them right now. And I resent it when other people attempt to furnish answers to me. I'm sure that they mean well, but it is just not helpful.

I keep being hit in the face by my inability to accept that you are dead, that I'll never see you again. I simply can't take that in. How can it be true? You were such a central part of my life. Now, I feel that my life has no core. My life has been exploded. There is nothing left but shards. Where am I? Where do I go? What do I do? When I think about how your live, conscious self would react to knowing that you are dead, I see you dissolving into tears. I see you saying, "You mean I won't get a chance to grow up?" I see you as inconsolable. As for me, I wanted to see my son develop into a man. I wanted to experience your growth with you, and to grow with you. I miss you terribly. My last recollections of you include your happy wave "hello" on Thursday and my kiss goodbye on Tuesday. And then you were gone. Only my memories of your final moments remain. The rest is a blur.

And then, decelerated to a crawl, I begin to climb slowly, and the questions, forever unanswered, begin anew… I am exhausted. Be well.

Love,
Dad

July 11, 1988

Dear Andrew,

I have joined a bereavement support group. All the members are there because they have lost children. What a strange phrase! It's as if we have merely misplaced our sons and daughters.

But I didn't know what else to do. I need a place where I can be comfortable talking about you, and about us, and particularly about what happened. Sure, I know. I can talk with my friends. Well, to some I can, but I need more. I need the companionship that comes only with shared experience, however horrible. And I need the understanding that comes only with shared pain. I need to know that others have felt what I feel, and that I'm not crazy, or perhaps more important, that I'm not alone.

Mostly, the others in the group lost their children a long time ago, but the leader said that there is one woman, Gael, whose daughter died a few days before you, who has not come for a little while. I look forward to meeting her.

Today is Leah's birthday, and she is 14. I have hardly seen her since the first few weeks after … well, after. She wanted me to come over to Mom's house a lot, and I went there as much as I could, but, after a few weeks, I found the expectations that inhabit that place too onerous. I am no longer the same person who used to live there, and I can never be that person again. Nor do I want to be that person. I hope Leah's OK. It's hard for me to tell. But, I'll have to come up with some other way to keep our relationship alive.

In the meantime, I have been going back to work for a few weeks. I haven't been able to show up quite on time, and I find that all I can manage is to sit and stare out my window, and then I leave early. I can't concentrate on my work yet—there are too many eddies of feeling, tinged with doubt, for me to begin even to think about technical research. Besides, of what importance is it, really? It's impossible for me to care. But, at least I've started to go. They have been wonderfully patient with me. When I hear what others who have had losses have experienced from their employers, I am overwhelmed with the kindness the people in my organization have shown me.

I don't know if I'll ever be able to care about work again, Andrew. After all, what does it matter? What little I do, when you have lost so much by comparison! Indeed, what does anything matter?

Look in on Leah …

Love,

Dad

July 22, 1988

Dear Andrew,

Monday night and Tuesday, I felt so depressed that I didn't care if I lived or died. By Tuesday night, when I went to my support group, I felt better, although still depressed. The group members all said that my depression was probably caused by the "anniversary". Tuesday was the 19th of the month, the second month after you were killed. I don't know, but I am scared when I feel so depressed. The people in the group also told me that anger and the need to blame are normal. They have all felt it. But, they said that my case seems complicated enough, that it would be confusing. It certainly is confusing to me. Sometimes I feel consumed by what I know, by my memories.

Thursday, Dale and I went to the cemetery. I couldn't remember where your grave was, and I panicked. I ran up and down looking for you, and I couldn't find you, but Dale was reassuring -- he knew where it was. I allowed him to calm me, and we sat there together for a while. Then, Dale walked around and left me to be alone with you. I just cried and felt sad. I couldn't seem to leave your side. I want to go back and stay with you, and so does Dale. And yet, in a strange way, I do not feel you there, in the cemetery. Little boys have no business in graveyards.

This morning, after I worked out, I felt the need to hit the punching bag and scream. I felt angry with the driver. I have had a fantasy that, at our camp this year, playing softball, I will hit the ball literally out of the world. (I have wondered what that is about for a while.) As soon as I began hitting the punching bag, I knew that it is the *driver* I want to hit out of the world. I want to hit him with the baseball bat and knock his head clean off. Then, the same for other people who hurt you. I screamed and hit and screamed some more. Then, I just broke down and cried, as I clung to the punching bag. Afterwards, I went upstairs and cried some more.

Crying used to be so difficult for me. I had worked so hard to reclaim my tears before, but now, I feel on the verge of crying all the time. We have paid too high a price for such a small victory.

I miss you, my little boy. Every cell in me misses you. I miss your little hands that I held in mine, and your little feet that I so often pushed into your shoes. I miss your hugs and smiles. I miss your attentiveness and I miss the way your hair flopped down over your forehead. I miss our snuggles, and I miss our fights. I miss your questions during movies, and I miss our man-to-man discussions. I miss your inquisitiveness, and I miss our adventures. I miss that sparkle in your eye, and, yes, I even miss your mischievous behavior. I miss your little giggles, and I miss your uncontrolled laughter. I miss playing baseball with you, and I miss playing Ping-Pong with you.

Something in me died with you, and everything is different. It can never be as though you never were. Perhaps it can be that you will live on in a special room in my heart, and yet, you were there when you were alive. Will I ever be fully alive again?

I miss you, my little boy.

Love,

Dad

August 5, 1988

Dear Andrew,

I miss you so much! I feel deprived of a son, my son, of all ages, 8 and up. The pain is systemic. I feel it all over, sometimes in my throat, sometimes in my head, sometimes in my stomach, sometimes all over. Sometimes, I feel it as despair. What does anything matter? Sometimes, I feel separate from my community. About those who know about you, I think, "He knows about my son, but he can't really know." About those who don't, I think, "He doesn't know about what has happened, and I don't want to tell him." Yet, when I shared my feelings with a coworker yesterday, I cried, I was angry, and I felt better. Sometimes I feel angry, so angry I swear I could kill, though I know in my heart that I couldn't.

My friends and I are in different places, yet how could anyone be in the same place as I am? Probably, I need to be more open about sharing where I am because people don't know what to say to me otherwise. I'm sure that I can easily communicate that I am OK and that I don't need anything from anyone, which is certainly not true.

Sometimes the pain is so intense that it takes my breath away and I have to fight to inhale. I have found that if I hold on to my anger, then I don't feel the pain, and if I let go of the anger, I immediately feel the pain -- deep, searing pain. Then, sometimes I have both.

I sense feelings all around me, flowing like jet streams, winds of fear and winds of anger, swirling all over. I feel them particularly strongly around people who interacted with you in those last days and weeks. The more I know about your last days, the more pain I feel for your life, and the less I want ever to have anything to do with those people. Those veritable storms caused such turbulence for you, and they threaten to distance me from the mourning I desperately need to do. After all, they keep me wrapped up in the aspects of life that now feel unimportant, unessential. Yet I sense them all over. They grow from little eddies and then they merge to form a powerful whirlpool, threatening to suck the life out of me. Perhaps, the only way to survive is to flow with it as long as necessary to build momentum and then slip out. No, that's what I've tried to do my whole life, and it's too hard to know when to slip out. It's best just to stay out of the storms in the first place.

Lately, my dreams of you are so real that they are more like visits than dreams. It seems that they usually happen in the almost morning hours, when you used to rouse yourself, and, in the aftermath, I don't know which is reality, dreaming or waking. I know which I prefer.

Last night's visit began with a big wrestle. You pushed me over onto my back, as you so often loved to do, and then you lay on my chest. I never knew when our wrestles just simply turned into snuggles, but at some point, I realized that we were rolling around, hugging and laughing. But, you stopped laughing and pulled up slightly. Holding yourself up by your arms, you looked at me more seriously.

Then, as you gazed lovingly, almost searchingly into my eyes, the strangest thing happened. The whole dream stopped. I don't mean that the dream ended, but it froze, like a video "pause". Your image became slightly grainy and the color drained out, like an old sepia photo. And yet, in the still silence of the moment, I felt the warmth of your breath, the weight of your body, the gentle pressure of your arms and hands. But, I saw deeply into your eyes, and you were distant, and I knew that I would never again hold you like that. I would never again see you like that. This was to be the last time.

But the feelings were so real. Your eyes, your face, your presence were so real. The dream woke me, but it felt as though it must have actually happened. Never again. It's far too long.

You know, I have told friends that I wish I had had one more hug, one more chance to say goodbye. Well, now, I guess I've had that chance, and it doesn't help. I still want to go back to last week, last month, even the beginning of the dream. Just give me that last hug one more time, and then again, and again … I guess it could never be enough.

I know, there's really nothing new to say. I've said how much I love you many times during your life, so I'm confident that you know. Maybe I could tell you how proud I have always been of you for your generosity and your kindness to others. Maybe I could tell you how much I have enjoyed you -- your humor, your delightful and endless questions, your sense of fun and adventure, and your creativity. Maybe I could tell you how much I learned from you. I must have told you these things before, but I can't remember. Haven't I told you? I wish I could remember more.

But that last hug -- if only I could just hold on forever! Maybe then you'd be safe. If only.

Love,
Dad

August 10, 1988

Dear Andrew,

Soon, it will be time for Camp Walden, and the original plan was that you would come, too. I can't imagine what camp will be like without you. How could I? I can't imagine what life will be like without you. I don't know how to describe how I feel most of the time, but I'll try.

Everything feels strange to me. The sidewalk beneath my feet feels different than ever before, and so do the air and the sun. It is as though I have become dislocated, and so I recognize the objects around me, but I experience them as altered. Perhaps I have been rotated 90 degrees part way into another dimension, so that I can still perceive things from my usual reality, but only at an angle. Perhaps I am walking around in a daze, and what I am feeling is the result of being in a dreamlike state. Perhaps my senses are overloaded from grief, and the majority of my nerve endings are simply numb. I don't know. I only know that I feel as though I have been transported in my sleep to a strange new planet that is bizarrely similar to the one I have inhabited all my life, but not after all, the same, and all of the residents of this copycat world are pretending to have known me for years. Come to think of it, though, even my own body feels strange to me. My hands, my feet, everything is somehow different.

I feel cut adrift. Nothing I do seems to give me pleasure or satisfaction. There are so many things I could do and yet, I don't feel like doing anything. My work, my art, my writing, nothing satisfies me. All feels empty. Sometimes I ask, "What am I here for?"

By the way, I met Gael from the support group and she is feeling the exact same way, so at least I'm not alone.

Maybe that's the key, at least I'm not alone. Somehow, that changes everything. As I wander around this off-world I seem to inhabit currently, I know that there is someone else from my home planet trying, like me, to return to the familiar. I wonder, maybe there is no return for us. Maybe we just have to learn to adjust to our new environment, both inside and out.

At Walden this year, I will be among the friends who have helped me survive these last few months. It will be good to share the week with them. I miss their closeness, but I also wonder if they will expect me to behave in a particular way because of your death. I have to say that this question comes from inside me -- no one else has even suggested such a thing. I have worried before in my life about what I think is expected of me. What is different for me now is that I don't think it matters to me. I have made it this far by being true to myself emotionally, and honest with myself, and with others. I expect to continue at Walden, whatever that will mean there.

Do you remember Linda? You met her last New Year's Eve at her house. I have found her very attractive for quite some time, and, this summer, I learned that she finds me attractive. We decided not to date right now, but she is coming to Walden this year, her first time, and, well, who knows what will happen?

Actually, in one way, I'm looking forward to Walden even more this year than ever before. I need the emotional intensity that camp provides. Intensity is certainly my internal reality, and it will be a relief to have my external surroundings match. I'll write to tell you how it went.

Love,
Dad

August 18, 1988

Dear Andrew,

The divorce was final, at last, just today. Oh, the paperwork will take some time, but the agreement was completed today. All the struggle we withstood since 1985, all the conflict we endured, is over. Oh, I'm sure there will be friction and unpleasantness ahead, but the major battles are finished. Before, there were two primary areas of contention, money and you. Now, of course, your custody, your welfare will never be an issue between Mom and me again. By contrast, money was not difficult to settle, at least with the help of some expected rulings on the part of the judge. After all, with money, the judge can follow guidelines, and that's just what she did.

So, it's over. I'm free, free to live without fear of an impending courtroom battle, free of lawyers and free of having to explain my actions and prove my motives, free of accusations, free of always having to tell people how the divorce is going, free to look back and start to heal. I'm not free to see you, though, and so this is a mixed experience at best. It shouldn't happen this way. The divorce should not have been easier for me to negotiate because of your death. Nothing should be easier.

I know that you never wanted the divorce. Probably no child ever wants to see his parents divorce. And I'm sure that it's no consolation that I feel I became a better father to you after the separation than I was before. Right now, that knowledge doesn't seem to comfort me either. You see, to me, your death was a part of the divorce, a consequence almost. I can't separate the two. It is an irony that the legal process is complete just one day shy of three months after your death, when three months or more ago, I would have said that there was no end in sight.

I remember the beginning. You and I had some rough times at first, after I moved out. I had been married to Mom for over 17 years, and now I had to learn how to manage a whole new life on my own. I didn't understand that you had to learn how to manage a whole new life as well. You were angry and I thought that I had to do something about it. In fact, I thought that I had to fix it. At the time, it sometimes seemed that we were so distant; we were miles apart from each other. I didn't figure out for some months that all I had to do was to listen to you and to accept your anger and your frustration. You just needed someone to hear you and to understand. After that, we became close again, perhaps closer than ever before.

Even during the difficult times, though, I knew that you needed me in your life. In the last year of your life, it became obvious to me just how much you needed me. In response, I became afraid that something might happen to me, and that you would be left without a father. Then, gradually, that fear changed and, in the two weeks before your death, I realized that I had become afraid that I would lose you.

How did this happen? What triggered the change? I'm not sure. Perhaps I sensed that you were vulnerable in some way. I'm not even sure when I became aware, but, by the last two weeks, I felt it. I think my first inkling came in a dream.

I dreamt that I was Macduff, from Shakespeare's Macbeth, and I had just been told that my whole family had been murdered, even the children. As in the play, half in shock, half in grief, the only thing I could say was, "All?" over and over. Even as I said it, though, I knew the truth, that all my children were gone. I awoke from the nightmare in a cold sweat. I had other dreams that worried me, but I couldn't remember them, just the feelings of dread they induced.

Then, the last Tuesday when you came over, I felt uneasy. I don't know how to describe it any other way. It was a vague sense of disquiet and apprehension, as if something was simply not right, but I couldn't place what it was. Do you remember what we talked about? I remember so clearly. I just *had* to talk to you about safety. We spoke about what to do if you found yourself on your bike, for example, and going out of control into a dangerous situation, like an intersection. We decided that the best thing might be simply to fall down as a way to stop. Oh, yes, it would hurt, but it would be far less painful than being hit by a car. And then I remember warning you not to play with Nate because I had seen you take risks while playing with Nate that I knew you would never take on your own. It was such a relief to me to be able to talk to you about these issues, and you listened. I know you did, because of your responses. This was not a parental lecture from me to you -- I know what those are like. It was a discussion, in which you showed genuine interest.

Later, I dropped you off at Mom's house, and you said the strangest thing. I said, "I'll see you on Thursday." and you replied, "Wanna bet?" It was not sassy, but more matter of fact. "Wanna bet?" In a moment, you were out of the car and into Mom's house. Those were the last words I ever heard you speak. I was surprised, too, because that kind of expression was not characteristic of you, or of us. I turned those words over in my mind for a while that night before I let it go. Since then, I have often wondered what energy, what spirit put those words on your lips that Tuesday night.

Then came the dream that night. I dreamt that I was driving you and Mom somewhere in a small red car. What car was that? Was it our old Chevette, sold these many years? And why was Mom with us? We were driving alongside a wood. The trees were bare and there was snow on the ground, so it must have been winter. Suddenly, we came to a clearing where a crowd was gathered, the people just milling around without visible purpose. I stopped and we got out to investigate. Mom disappeared into the crowd and we never saw her again. At that point, someone with a commanding view of the clearing opened fire with a machine gun, killing many people in the crowd. There was chaos! People were running everywhere, trying to get away. You and I were crouched next to the car, and I told you to stay behind me. You disobeyed me, though, and the next I knew, the man with the machine gun had captured you. I was terrified! I knew that he intended to kill you, and I had to do something to stop him. I stood up to divert his attention, and, at the same time, I yelled for you to run for it. I saw him train his weapon on me, as you broke free and jumped down the roadside embankment. I awoke with the feeling of bullets ripping through my body, and the dismal knowledge that my sacrifice had been in vain. You would be killed anyway.

It was Wednesday morning when this dream put an abrupt end to my night's rest. I didn't know then how soon my days and nights would change forever.

That day, while driving to work, I thought I might have hit a bird. There was a group of birds clustered around something in the road and I slowed as much as I could, while the flock dispersed. I wasn't sure, but I thought I heard a "thump" at the same time that my peripheral vision identified a dark trajectory that was noticeably too low to clear the car. "Well," I thought, "perhaps I was wrong." However, as I was refilling my gas tank, I examined the front of the car for any signs of what might have happened on the way in. I was shocked and disturbed to find the body of a dead bird caught in the grillwork. I had never hit an animal before, not in the 26 years I had been driving. Now, I felt at least partially responsible for the death of this innocent creature. Even if I didn't do anything overtly "wrong", this bird's death was part of the cost paid for my lifestyle, for my mobility. My sadness stayed with me for the rest of Wednesday.

The next day, Thursday, when I came to pick you up, you were playing with Nate ... A moment later, you lay in the street, dead. How I wish you had done what I told you to do! How I wish ...

How many times I have wondered what, if anything, your last words meant. What did my dreams and fears mean? What energy conspired to warn me but then leave me powerless? Is there, in fact, a story behind the story? Indeed, is there meaning in events, or, is all just madness?

Now the ball of yarn in which I had been tangled since at least 1985 is completely unraveled, and there seem to be no new knots to snag me in the future. It is as though, these last years, I inhabited a tornado, spinning, spinning, sweeping everything in its path until, abruptly, and with no warning, it just dissipated. The voracious storm simply vanished into a wisp of dust, leaving the air clear and calm. I am bewildered at this unexpected tranquility when I have become accustomed to such a turbulent existence.

What a swath this particular tornado has cut into our lives, however! We may be able to clean the debris and rebuild some of what has been destroyed, but true repair is not possible. The wounds are too deep. The scars are permanent.

Am I relieved that the divorce is settled? Yes, sadly I am. Will I miss you forever? Absolutely.

Love,
Dad

September 1, 1988

The next letter is about a camp experience at a workshop called "Walden". It was a unique place and it was a pivotal experience for me each of the four years I attended. Two of them were with Andrew. From the brochure for Walden, "a gentle adventure in living community":

"The Walden Summer Workshop is a week-long workshop, held at a summer camp, for people of all ages and in any combinations (singles, couples, families, friends, etc.). It is a week of living and playing together, a week of creating a community which is supportive and cooperative, and which thereby fosters the personal growth of each participant.

"The concept and total experience of Walden rest on values such as love, inner peace, inter-personal trust and cooperation, responsibility for self and others, emotional sharing and connectedness ...

"Some of the experiential goals of the Walden Summer Workshop are: acknowledgment of our own and others' personal growth and presence; risk-taking in areas such as self-expression, intimacy, physical and creative activity; a heightened appreciation of nature; meeting and cooperatively interacting with others as persons, without age, sex or role preconceptions; discovery and sharing of creative capacities; and just plain fun and relaxation. It is our hope that these are valued life goals for all of us, and that the structure and program of the week engage us in mutual cooperation toward the achievement of these goals ...

"In addition to the ongoing availability of camp recreational facilities, the week typically includes Humanistic Sports and New Games, a crafts program, tubing and water play, square dancing, a talent show, 'brown bag' intimacy lunches, an American Indian ceremonial campfire, special programming for kids, and some all-group gatherings."

Dear Andrew,

Sometimes, years later, we look back on an experience and we realize that that event was a pivotal point in our lives. Somehow, at the time, we don't notice. It takes the perspective of distance and perhaps further growth before we can appreciate what actually transpired in that critical moment. On the other hand, sometimes, we know right away, even as our encounter with fate evolves, that we will never be the same. Your death was certainly like that for me. This year, in a positive way, Walden was like that for me.

I have been home from Walden for about a week and I feel transformed compared to the week before camp. Oh, no, I'm not done mourning. Not at all. I took my grief with me to Walden and I brought it home again. What I think is different is that I'm no longer grieving exclusively. When I left for Walden, I wasn't sure how committed I was to living, really living. I wasn't sure if anything in life could be important to me again. Now I know that there are things in life that are terribly important to me. How did this happen? Well, I don't know, exactly. What I do know is that, by midweek, I felt infused with new life energy, an unaccustomed spirit of belonging and a renewed sense of purpose.

I guess, my new Walden experiences started soon after arrival. Indeed, I have always been shy about singing in public, so I was surprised when I found myself singing "Black Socks" alone, in front of the whole group, at the campfire that first Sunday night. Then, after I sang, I taught "Black Socks" to the group and led them in rounds. Do you remember the song? You had performed it in school and then taught it to me, so I wanted to hear it around the campfire as a way of connecting to you. Even with that strong motivation, however, I was terrified even to volunteer, much less to begin. But, once I started singing, I lost myself in the song. It was as if I was unobserved, and I found that my anxiety evaporated. This was the first of many activities in which I took a risk and then immersed myself completely, as if I had always done it this way. Well, you know how Walden is -- filled with activities that can be fun, but are often challenging. I guess the object is to explore, and even to expand your personal boundaries.

I'll tell you more about what I did by and by, but before I do, I want to relate some interpersonal exchanges that were both puzzling and deeply meaningful to me. From the very beginning of camp, and throughout the week, people sought me out to share their fears, particularly the fear of caring, and then being hurt. The first person who singled me out in private related her fear of investing in the camp experience itself, because of how she might feel when she left. I had two reactions, both of them honest reflections of my own feelings. Certainly, I understood. Whenever we have a choice and one decision carries the risk of pain, we are tempted to go with the other option. Simultaneously, however, my inner voice screamed, "No! You live it and then mourn the passing of it when it is over." Where did this come from? Had this determination always been a part of me, but only loosed by my journey of recent months? And yet, during this time, without realizing it, I had been living out the essence of that powerful conviction. Later, others came to me to share their dread of investing in relationships, for fear of being hurt, and I had the same internal reaction as before. Each one had come to this place from their own well of loss and grief, and I began to see their question as a universal one: how do you commit your heart when you know how badly it can be hurt? I certainly understand.

Now, it was clear to me that these conversations were not haphazard. These people did not chance to encounter me at the very moment they felt the urge to talk about their fear. No, they specifically sought me out to share an issue that had been bothering them for some time. How ironic that they should approach me, who had been struggling with the fundamental question: is there anything in this life worth doing or having? I wonder, is this a different question from theirs? Yet their doubt, their fear, had ignited the flame of resolution in my own soul. And I found myself not just knowing, but doing.

At first, on Monday, I struggled with rapid transitions between such extremes of feeling. The opening activity was a scavenger hunt, followed by a skit, and I became deeply involved. I enjoyed Linda's creative ideas and the group energy. I even lost myself in the performance, but then I broke down afterwards, as Dale held me. I just kept questioning, how could I be so fully engaged when you're not here, and will never be here? Then, somehow, as with the passing of a cloudburst, violent, but short-lived, I was all right and ready to rejoin the group. The next activity was a form of directed dancing, and I lost myself in the rhythm and the movement. Immediately after, as before, I broke down sobbing, as Alex held me, and my thoughts embraced your absence. Again, I recovered and rejoined the group. Later, I danced with Linda and enjoyed our closeness. I walked her back to her cabin and then, after, I went down to the lake, where, in previous Walden years, you and I liked to play together. I sat alone on the end of the dock, and my tears mingled with the lake water. It was a deeper sadness than I felt earlier, but with less distress, and I was comfortable sharing it with the night breeze.

As I write this, I see that what I was doing, without thinking about it, was that I was losing myself in whatever was going on, inside and out. It was a form of commitment to just being—the deepest form of investing. I was certainly unaware that evening, however.

At the same time, I was enjoying my time with Linda, and I felt my attraction was intensifying, but I did not yet appreciate where we were going. Sometimes, it is better for the traveler to keep an eye on the road without unduly anticipating the destination, or without even trying to read the map.

The next day, the group activity involved making our own musical instruments, using common craft materials, and I thought of Leah. How I miss her! Only one year ago, she shared the week here with you and me, and, at the talent sharing, we all enjoyed her beautiful violin performance. With Leah on my mind, I wanted to build a stringed instrument of some sort and ultimately, I fashioned a crude "lyre". Once again, I had immersed myself in my activity. At the end, I was sad, but not devastated as on Monday. The time had passed effortlessly, with no hint of the changes that were going on inside me. If I had to describe my general mood that day, I might have said that I felt half contemplative, almost as though one eye was observing the world around me while the other had turned inward. That night, as I lay in bed, I gazed at the ceiling, intent on taking some time to relive and process the day, but instead, I was overtaken by an intense, dreamless sleep.

Wednesday morning, seemingly moments later, I awoke early, feeling truly alive and free, more so than ever before in my life. What does this mean? I'm not describing a feeling of bliss or even happiness. No, this emotion is closer to passion—the passion to experience and to be in the world, the passion to know and to be known, whatever comes! I dressed quietly so as not to disturb my still slumbering friends and I emerged from my cabin into semi-darkness. Here, I found Lindsey, who, defying the apparent natural tendency of teenagers to sleep late, had arisen before anyone else. So, I was the second one up. I have felt a special bond with Lindsey at camp this year because of the time he took with you at the holiday party last winter. I often recall the scene of the two of you on the floor, he sharing his drawing talents with you, and you soaking it up gratefully. Now that seems another time, another life, ago.

In this time, Lindsey and I walked east, out the woods road to the clearing, where we celebrated the dawning of Walden's midweek. The early rays of light, filtering through the surrounding boughs, chased shadow from the open field and set the early morning dew asparkle. It promised to be a beautiful day. And so it was! And I was acutely aware of every detail of it.

Later, Richard approached me about performing a vision quest with the goal of providing direction for a memorial service for you. I remember, last year at Walden, you were fascinated by Richard's annual Native American ceremony and you willed yourself to stay awake until the end. Then, overcome with fatigue because of the late hour, you took yourself off to bed. I remember feeling proud of you for showing such independence. I had never before participated directly in the ceremony, but this year, I felt the need to connect with you spiritually, as well as emotionally. The ceremony seemed like the place to do that.

To start, I was to find a stone that was, in some way, meaningful to me. Later, I would identify an animal that I could relate to you. It would be misleading to describe the quest itself as an activity, because that word almost implies a kind of conscious direction. No, by contrast, I was to go about it in, what is for me, a whole new way. I was to continue with my normal camp activities (that word again!), and, seemingly, to let the stone find me. Wednesday afternoon, my quest began.

By the way, I want you to know that the children at camp, who all knew you from previous Waldens, have been wonderful. They have been reaching out to me, writing lovely messages about you and about us, and giving lots of hugs. How must they, who are so young, relate to your loss? I cannot imagine. Sometimes, though, I feel their eyes keenly upon me, if only from a distance, and I sense that what they want to see is both that I grieve and that I am surviving, both that I care so much for you that I am broken hearted and that yet, I have enough spirit to still share love. It is almost as though they look to me for leadership in how to feel such loss and yet live. I hope I do not disappoint.

I have been watching Linda, and I love seeing her with the children -- she loves kids. I love seeing her relating to my friends, doing her art, being creative and having fun. As we agreed we would before Walden, Linda and I have taken time to share whatever feelings arise between us -- even feelings of insecurity. I think that this is actually bringing us closer. I told Dale that I could fall in love with Linda, and he said, "It's too late. You already have." Could it be so? Are we so much more visible to outside observers than to ourselves? Could it be that I had been so enamored of following the process that I neglected to notice that it was past? Later, I was to learn from others that Linda and I were the last ones to perceive the truth about ourselves. Perhaps, instead of falling in love, we went through the journey of discovering that we already were.

Oh, yes, I found a stone, or one found me, and something about it, shape or essence, suggested "bear". With fresh memories of your joyous running, whether at soccer or with kite in tow, I named you Little Running Bear. I hope you like your Native American name.

The shield consists of a leather "canvas", stretched over a circular wooden frame. Linda would paint the leather with different symbols suggested by my friends who knew you best. An evergreen tree would symbolize the permanent effect your short life had on all who knew you. A cactus with a single flower would symbolize your struggle to blossom, even under harsh circumstances. A bow and arrow set against the sun would recall your love for archery and your hope for the future, and a bird would symbolize your coming to a place where you could begin to soar. In the center would be a bear, warm and cuddly, like you. Tied to the shield would be five stones and five feathers, one of them an eagle's feather.

The shield was to be presented to me at your memorial, on Saturday night, and that would be the first time I would see it completed. I had no idea how the ceremony would feel to me, but collaborating with Linda and my other friends on planning the shield was an intense experience. After all, how often do we stop to contemplate and try to capture the essence of someone we love so completely? How much rarer it is that our dearest friends so willingly assist!

On Friday morning, we had an all-camp meeting to welcome those who came for the final weekend and to integrate our experiences thus far. I felt that I had changed so much since arrival on Sunday! Was that really only five days ago? But, I was not the only one who had been affected so powerfully by this Walden. Many of my friends shared their own growth and change. I was particularly moved that, this year, the children chose to express themselves so openly and lovingly, and I wondered what, if anything, you would have had to say. Maybe you would have been too shy to speak. I don't know.

At the end, Roz played "The Garden Song", and the words flew directly to my soul. They formed a metaphor, a prayer, every parent's prayer, to bless what I have sown and yet I know that this prayer is not always answered. Here, in this very room, sat so many beautiful children. Why could not mine have been here as well? My vision began to blur, as the phrases echoed in my heart over and over – the rhymes begging, please, for someone to protect the helpless until they can fend for themselves, and I could no more hold back the tears than will myself to stop breathing. I became aware of the sound of enormous sobs and I suddenly realized they were coming from me. I found myself lying on the floor as Linda held me, her cheeks wet with sorrow, and the whole group gathered around us, hugging, crying, caring. Time stopped in deference to teardrops. You are missed more than you know.

Eventually, my well ran dry. Now, even as I write this, I am in a daze. How much more so at the time! But then, I also felt a deep sense of quiet. All that I had to say had been said, more eloquently than language can devise, however artful, and I felt peaceful, as if finally having settled a long-outstanding debt. There is comfort in grief shared that is denied the solitary mourner. I'm sure that I will learn this lesson anew, time and again.

The rest of Friday proceeded at a slower pace, it seemed. I committed to reading Steven Vincent Benet's "The Mountain Whippoorwill", in the talent sharing that night. It is a poem about a Hillbilly boy who grows up alone in Georgia, with nothing but a fiddle made of mountain laurel-wood. It is the story, in his own words, of his winning the great fiddlers' prize at the Essex County Fair. It's a dramatic poem, with deep personal meaning for me -- I often feel the outsider, like the Hillbilly at the fair with "all the smarty fiddlers from the South".

Performing it would not be easy. Yet, when the time came, I melted into the role, "an' -- they wasn't no crowd to get me fazed ... but I was alone where I was raised." My speech lapsed into the Kentucky twang that I heard so frequently during my three years living in the South, and I whispered, I sang, I yelled, I trembled, and ... I did it. For those moments, I was the Hillbilly, fiddling for all he was worth. And when I was done, well, "then the noise of the crowd began". Now, as the exhilaration fades, I wonder, how is it that such highs and such lows as I have felt can coexist within one person? Are these in fact opposing factions, or are they really different expressions of the same underlying passion, like distinct facets of a complex prism?

The next day, Saturday, was to be the last full day of Walden. At breakfast, we all commented on the rare and persistent hoots from the owls that awakened us that morning. Later that night, we would all attend the dinner banquet, followed by the Ceremonial Campfire, with your memorial. It was a day of quiet preparation for many of us. Linda spent most of the day painting your shield. She also painted one for Jared, for a ceremony to welcome him to the world. I remember that only a few months ago, you picked out a silver baby spoon as a gift for his baby shower. I knew that this would be a painful juxtaposition for me -- a ceremony for a beginning next to one for an ending, an indescribably sad event adjoining a joyous one.

In the afternoon, I found myself alone and feeling contemplative, in a field away from the center of camp. In my daily routine, I often think of you and I sometimes speak to you, at least in my head. This felt different. I felt as though I could almost touch you here, beneath this canopy of blue, surrounded by pillows of green. Surely, if I spoke aloud in such a place, then you could hear me. Surely, if you heard me, then you would listen. And surely, if you listened, then you would understand. I need you to understand.

I lay on my back, my arms open to the universe, and I called out to you, "Andrew, I need to tell you something about myself and it's important. It's also hard for me, but I have to tell you anyway. I have some life to live yet, and I want to truly live every minute of it. It's not that I need to forget about you, or even to stop mourning. Quite the contrary! I wouldn't even call this, 'moving on'. But, I need to discover the life I was meant to lead. I need to climb my own tree, now more than ever." For a while, I felt no response, and then, slowly, I became aware of a sense, starting somewhere in my chest and then spreading throughout my body and finally to my brain, that it was all right with you. I continued to lie prostrate, basking in gentle vibrations and sinking slowly downward into the endless sky. At least for now, all my warring dissidents were at truce.

At the ceremony that night, Richard explained that the owls we all heard in the morning signified the presence of spirits, according to Native American belief. And so you were present. You were present when Louise read a passage from "The Little Prince". It was the one in which the prince makes a deal with the snake to bite him, so he can leave his heavy body behind and travel back to his home planet. I have often wondered if you made some kind of deal with the snake, and hence your final words, "Wanna bet?" I wish I knew. In the story, the prince leaves a gift for his friend, the aviator, namely the knowledge that one of the stars will shelter the prince and there, he is laughing. Because the aviator won't know which star the prince inhabits, it will be as if all the stars are laughing. I thought of the prince taming the fox, who then weeps when it is time to part. It seems that weeping a little is one of the risks of allowing oneself to be tamed. You have tamed me, and, in your presence, I wept. You were present when Richard announced your new name, Little Running Bear, and handed me the shield, crafted with symbols of love from our dear friends. You were present when Richard asked me to dance and I took my first tentative steps. And then, just you and I were present as I lost myself in movement, never touching the ground, just soaring, spinning, flying gracefully … free! And then it was over, Little Running Bear. The rest recorded itself as a blur in my memory.

Linda and I stayed close the rest of the evening. I love her smile. I love how beautiful she is. I love her openness to people. I want to be more open myself, so I admire that quality in her. We shared so very much with each other this week. We shared fears, as well as caring and admiration. We were honest, and we were vulnerable. And we are changed. By Sunday, Linda and I both knew what everyone else had known all along -- we love each other. What's next for us? We'll see after Walden.

In the past, at Walden's end, I have mourned the passing of the week. This year, I haven't. I lived each day as it came and I'm taking Walden with me. Interestingly, on parting, a number of people told me how much they learned from me. From me! I'm not sure what it could be.

Now, in retrospect, I realize that I don't give myself credit for what is truly difficult, like: just going to Walden, never mind the risks I took there; or, just attempting the poem at talent-sharing, never mind the manner in which I performed it; or, just engaging in a vision quest, never mind dancing with the shield. I also realize that, of all the risks I took, the biggest was being willing to love again.

No doubt, there will be more depression and much more grief, but even that is just part of the process. I want to live intensely and fully, whatever that means at the time. Right now, that includes being in love with Linda. I miss you.

Thanks for understanding.

Love,

Dad

October 2, 1988

Dear Andrew,

I miss you so terribly much. I think about you constantly, and I feel an ache all over. Two weeks ago, on Monday, it was your birthday. Happy birthday! I stayed home from work to be with you, and with me. I watched "Superman, The Movie" and I thought of you, of how much you loved that movie. I cried when I thought of all the things that Superman could do, that I wished I could have done to save you on that horrible Thursday. Remember, after Pa Kent died, Clark said that even with all of his powers, he still couldn't save his father? That's how I often feel. In spite of all my talents and skills, I couldn't save you. I had begun to comprehend that before you died, too. In spite of the energy I was willing to expend for you, no matter what I was willing to do, I couldn't necessarily make things come out right. However, knowing is not a balm for the pain. Understanding is often not a consolation.

Do you remember the part in the movie when Clark Kent first changes into Superman so he can save Lois Lane? I played that part over and over, wishing I could have changed and flown just in time to snatch you from the street that day. Then, oh then, we would have talked about your close call! Why then, we would have had the rest of the day, no, the rest of our lives, to talk about it and to marvel. But, I could not change and then fly to you in time, and so I played that part of the movie again and wished.

Later, on your birthday, I flew a kite, a large bird kite, and I talked to you. Some of the boys in the neighborhood came to see what I was doing. A lot of the children who knew you have been very kind and supportive toward me. That shows me how much they cared about you, about us. I will always love you and I will always ache for your absence. But I want always to have a relationship with you. I want always to be able to stop and talk to you. So many aspects of my life were tied up with you, and I want them always to be.

After Walden, I had the photos developed, including some that were left in the camera from before. I was shocked to find that there were pictures of your 8th birthday party. I had not remembered that I had taken them. Your last birthday went so beautifully! Do you remember? We had a group of your friends over for dinner, cake and ice cream, and Dale came over to help out. Then, we had a treasure hunt and the clues were written in code. Both groups ended up in the backyard, where Dale was blowing enormous bubbles. The prize for each boy was a water gun, and we all shot out the bubbles in the air. What made it so special was that you and all your friends seemed to be having so much fun. Later, you took time to play with each gift, as if honoring its presence in your life. That was your way.

As much pleasure as it gives me to recall that day a little over a year ago, I am sad. These photos are your last. There will never be another. Photographs are a way we have of marking time and recording changes, and remembering. For you, there is no time to mark. There will be no changes to record. It is truth, I know, but I cannot grasp it.

One of the photos that was developed shows the portraits of you and of Leah that are hanging on my den wall. For some reason, the flash reflected off of the glass on yours, giving your likeness a special aura, almost like a halo. Was it an omen, stored safely in the camera against an incomprehensible future? Was it fate that guided my hand to point the camera just so? Sometimes, that seems possible. I have put together an album of all your photographs. It is short, too short. I have added the one with the aura. It is, and will be, the last picture in your collection.

You know, Andrew, there is something else I want to tell you, to discuss with you. It has been bothering me for a while. I don't know if you've noticed, but I have grown a lot since you died, and I like how I've grown. What I don't like is that I feel that things would have gone more slowly for me if you were still alive. I want to be who I am today, and I want you to be alive. Your death changed the course of my life forever. Part of me wishes that I would dislike everything that has happened as a result of your dying. But that isn't so. My reaction to your death has been to reach outside myself to other people in a way I never did before. I feel connected to people more deeply than ever before in my life. As I discovered at Walden, I feel more alive than ever before. At Walden, I learned that I am a passionate person, someone who experiences wide extremes of feeling, and I want to feel and express those extremes to the limits of my capability. Perhaps, that's what life is about for me. It is so physical and emotional, as well as intellectual and spiritual. I guess I was working on making these changes even before you died. I hope you like them. Somehow, I feel that you do.

Since Walden, I have been dating Linda, and we are more and more in love. Actually, I think that this has been coming for a long time. In fact, some of our friends have said that we finished falling in love at Walden. She is wonderful! I'm sure you would really love her, too. You know, this is a different feeling than I have ever had before. Did I mention that she is wonderful? Oh, and I can tell that she does not try to come between us. Quite the contrary! This is terribly important to me -- there is lots of room in our relationship for my relationship with you.

I miss you, Andrew. I love you always. I'll be talking to you.

Love,
Dad

October 19, 1988

Dear Andrew,

It is five months to the day since you were killed. One month ago today, it was your birthday, and the intervening time has been so very hard for me. I miss you. I love you. I have been talking to you some. I'll never know why you went into the street that day. I'll never know why the driver of the car didn't hit his brakes before he hit you. I'll just never know. That hurts, although it makes no difference to me to know anymore. It just feels sad to me. But it wouldn't bring you back to life. That's what I would really want, to bring you back to life unhurt.

As I write this passage, I realize that sometimes I feel that I'll never know, and that it doesn't matter to me, but, I also know that, other times, I feel obsessed with knowing. And further, sometimes I feel that, in fact, I know what happened, that there was a hidden story, and that I either know it or that I can figure it out. Certainly, my support group has confirmed that the situation is, at the very least, confusing. So, what do I need? What would make a difference? I don't know, but it is clear to me that I am not at peace with it, not at all.

I have felt so much loss these last weeks. First, I have lost you. Then, I began to feel the pain from everything else that I have ever lost—girlfriends, my marriage, and friends. I have lost my childhood. I have begun to feel the pain that comes from every corner of my life, from my teenage years, my early years, and my young adulthood. I have felt so much sadness all my life.

I realized this morning, as I drove to work, that there has never been anything that I wanted to do that I did not expect that I could just do. Of course, it could be that I have never really "wanted" to do anything truly challenging. I don't know. What I do know is that whatever talents I may have, I also have limits. It's hard for me to own it, but it's true. I wonder, is it all right for me to have limits?

I am so sleepy that I have to go to bed. I love you always. I'll talk to you soon.

Love,
Dad

PS: Leah seems to be doing all right. We have been seeing each other regularly. She is a beautiful young lady and I love her so very much. As close as the two of you were, I'm sure that you must miss each other terribly.

March 12, 1989

Dear Andrew,

It has been such a long time since I have written to you, but I think of you every day. I love you and I miss you terribly. Spring is coming. Remember last spring when you learned to play baseball?

I have been having such a hard time. It is nearly a year since the day you were killed. I can still say, "A year ago today, Andrew was still alive," but pretty soon I won't be able to say that. I have been remembering so vividly the day you were killed, and the weeks after. I remember how hard it was for me to confront your tearful face and tell you that you're dead, that you were hit by a car and killed. I remember ...

Last night, I had a dream. I have had lots of dreams about you. Last night I dreamt that you and I were in California together. I guess we were visiting. We were going to go for a drive in the car but I could not find our car. I was even confused about whether it was a 2-door or a 4-door car. I began to think that somehow it was stolen. After we walked around the parking lot for a while, though, we found it. Then, I had a difficult time getting you to wear your seat belt. You wanted to sit up a look around. That felt strange to me because it was always so important to you that you wear your seat belt whenever the car was in motion. In my dream, I imagined that, without your seat belt on, you could be hurt in case we stopped suddenly. I pictured you flying forward, in slow motion, head first through the windshield. In my dream, I thought, "I can't stand to see you killed again!" I didn't share that thought with you, but I got you (reluctantly) to put on your seat belt. Then, we went for a drive in a field full of beautiful daisies. It was lovely, and we stopped to get out to feel the fresh wind, and to smell the smells. As you walked around the front of the car, another car pulled up fast and stopped just next to and beyond us. You nearly got hit, but you pulled back and you flashed me one of your familiar looks that said, "Whew, close call!" This is all so hard for me to write. It just feels so painful, that it has me gasping for breath. Then, for some reason, I was in the back seat of my car, and the people from the other car were in my car eating custard donuts, and making a mess. I became enraged, and I told them to leave. They acted as though they had every right to be there, but they left. You and I looked at each other, as if to say, "Some strange people!" It reminds me of how you used to roll your eyes sometimes when you felt that you were being imposed upon. The dream didn't end there exactly. I don't know what else happened, but I awoke with the impression of you and with the sensation of all those beautiful flowers near by. I feel so sad today and I miss you so much. I can hardly believe it, but I realized yesterday that you would be almost 10 years old now.

Some days ago, I dreamt that I was coming to pick you up at Mom's. As I drove up to the house and slowed to turn into the driveway, you stopped playing with the other children and waved to me from the sidewalk. Then, there were just the two of us, you on the sidewalk and me in the car, and I heard you in my heart saying goodbye. As a reflex, I said goodbye, too, and at the same time, I cried out that I am not ready to say goodbye! I'm just not ready.

I have been sleeping restlessly, even when I don't remember my dreams, and I awake tired, no matter how long I stay in bed. My dreams of you are so vivid, that I don't want to wake from them. I want to stay with you -- even in the dreams where I have warned you about what would happen and I could tell it will do no good.

Sometimes, I have a hard time letting the outside world in, like now, but sometimes, I have let it in more than ever before. Either way, I am having a hard time. Sometimes, it just hits me between the eyes -- I just can't believe you're dead.

Listen, Andrew, I have also been doing more in the last months. I want to tell you about what else is going on for me. I have become involved in developing a new robot control algorithm, and sometimes I am really excited about it. It feels good to be excited again! The new algorithm is based on an idea that came out of a computer game you played at my office, the game in which you had to drive a car on a mountain road. The point is that it has sustained my interest and enthusiasm for the first time since I can remember. In addition, Leah and I have been seeing each other lately. We go out to dinner together and, sometimes, she comes over to my house for help with math. She gives me so much joy!

The other day, at work, I asked Sam how his children are doing. I haven't been able to do that before now. Since the divorce, I just haven't been able to. Then, when he told me, I just hurt so much. Erica is 8 years old, as you were when you were killed. Her picture sits on his desk and, when I looked at it, I saw your face instead of hers. I wanted to run away. You were dead! It was as though I was watching you die all over again and sometimes I feel I can't bear it.

Almost 2 months ago, Grandpa died. Somehow, I feel different since then. I feel liberated, but sadder. I understand a lot of things about my family better, and I feel less angry with my family than I did before. I have even talked to Grandma about it. Somehow, I feel freer to reach out to more people than before.

I have been feeling more and more in love with Linda, and, although it frightens me, I have been thinking about marrying her and, perhaps, having a family with her. That would mean more children, maybe even another son. I want you to know in your heart that no one could ever replace you. I will always have a special feeling for you, a special place for you in my heart.

I am having such a hard time with all of these intense feelings that seem so opposite each other. I enjoy such excitement about Linda, about Leah and about my work, and I suffer such pain and loss and emptiness because of your death. And I still ache with anguish when I imagine your pain, your tears, your loss. I feel helpless to do anything for you. I can't even hold you as you cry. Can we cry together in some way? Sometimes, I don't know how to tolerate these extremes of emotion, and then I need to be alone.

Today, I have been angry, angry with the driver who killed you, angry as hell with the boy who pushed you and angry with his family, angry with Mom, and even angry with you. Yes, you went into the street and got hit, and you left me here to remember and to mourn. And, yes, sometimes I can't stand it. Oh, if only I could tell you in person.

I love you, son. I miss you so much.

Love,

Dad

April 26, 1989

Dear Andrew,

God, this is hard! I have been feeling so empty without you. I have begun to understand at a deep level that I will never see you again. I can't stand that thought. I have been aching with such acute and constant pain, and I can't even begin to describe those sensations. But it is doing something to me. I feel changed. I am changing. It may not be the only thing going on in my life, but it underlies everything else. Even my enthusiasms are touched by it.

Today, I wanted to write to you about something positive. I wanted to write to you to tell you about our algorithm. Yes, our algorithm! Yours and mine! I have been so very excited about it. It is so neat. I don't know if anyone else can appreciate how I experience it. Do you remember when you came to visit me at the office and we went to the robot lab? I mentioned it in a previous letter, but let me remind you a little more about it. Well, Loran fixed you up with a computer game where you had to drive a car as fast as you dared on a mountain road and you tried to stay on the road and not hit anything. I remember it like it was yesterday. You had a lot of fun, I think. We talked about it later, on the way home. Well, that picture stayed on my mind, and later, after you were killed, it became the way for me to think about the new robot path planner. For years, I had been thinking about the problem of planning robot paths that made the hand follow a straight line, but I could not get far. Together, however, you and I made the breakthrough.

The idea is that, when you drive a car, you determine how fast you can go by road conditions, both immediate and future, and by how far ahead you can see to ascertain future conditions. This approach is so basic, so sensible, it's almost instinctive. Even an 8-year old, namely you, adopts this strategy. Each of the driving factors -- conditions on the road and the horizon of visibility -- has an analog in robot path planning. So, you see, the metaphor of driving on the road has enabled us to construct a strategy for controlling robots.

The algorithm is nearly done now, and when it is, perhaps Diana and I will try to patent it. I want you to know that you helped to invent it. That makes you an inventor, too. I know that you would be so pleased. I wish I could see your face when you knew. I wish I could see your face. The algorithm goes far beyond anything I dreamed of before. It has great power and flexibility. And it works. It's incredible! You're incredible. And now there is a part of you in my daily work.

I miss you. I love you.

Love,

Dad

May 5, 1989

Dear Andrew,

In two weeks, it will have been one year since you were killed, and I have no idea how that milestone will hit me now. I do know that I have been stuck in my grief. I think that I have not wanted to experience my anger about your death. Sadness, even pain, that's all right, but my anger has frightened me, so, until now, I have been able to keep it below the level of consciousness. In the meantime, in my outside life, the one the rest of the world sees, anger seems to be over a distant horizon. After all, my work is going well and Linda and I are talking of marriage.

In fact, she is going to move in to my house, our house. I wonder how that will go! I know that I'll have to make many adjustments. After all, she has furniture, too. She has to be able to call this house her home, too. I know that we won't be changing your room, though, so that's not a problem. I do need to get her a garage door opener for her car, but I have no idea where to go. Sometime, I'll have to look up the company listed on the back of my opener, and find their address, a small detail in my busy life these days.

Well, this is all a prologue to tell you about an incredible event that happened yesterday. It recalled something that happened when you were about 3 years old, and, while I'm sure you remember it, I want to tell you my recollection before I tell you about the event yesterday, because it reminds me that we have always been close, not just since a year ago.

This memory is from a time when I was still married to Mom. Yes, you were about 3, and you loved to climb. And you were so strong, and so confident, that you were very good at it. I remember that it was a beautiful summer day, and I was preparing to mow the lawn. I tell you, I hated to mow the lawn! Between the odor of gasoline fumes, and the flying grass and dust, and the insects, I just wanted to finish as fast as possible. But the worst part of mowing the lawn was the noise. I have to protect my hearing in my one good ear, and the roar of the engine always caused my head to ring. So, this time, I decided to shield my ears from the din by wearing a set of headphones. I could even listen to music during my unpleasant chore, and perhaps that would make the time pass more quickly.

So, there I was, merrily chugging around the backyard, listening to the radio and blissfully unaware that anyone else might even be nearby, when I heard a small, high voice inside my head, saying, "Help." Now, this was the strangest sensation, because the voice was not yelling, and I knew that I could not, in fact, be hearing such a sound. But, there it was again, "Help." It was said in a matter-of-fact tone, with no trace of panic, and again, "Help." I could not understand, so I stopped the lawnmower and heard it again, still over the sound of the radio, but oddly enough, no louder than before. Then, I took off the headset, and I heard you, in the same manner and with the same volume, say, "Help." I turned around, and you were hanging by your hands from the ladder that went across the top of the swing set. You could go no further. Nor could you just drop without hitting a swing and hurting yourself. So there you had been, calling, "Help." Impossibly, I had heard you. I ran over and got you down, but I never understood.

How could this have happened? My strict scientific explanation of phenomena had always precluded the possibility of this kind of event. And yet, it had happened to me, or rather, to us. I began to realize that I had become a mathematician in the first place because I wanted answers, straightforward answers at that. What a joke on me! Now I was learning that sometimes, or maybe often, life's mysteries simply cannot be explained by traditional math and science, especially where people are concerned.

So, there you have it. We have always been closely connected in some fundamental way that I have never been able to explain to anyone. Perhaps that is why I have felt you with me so much since you died. For example, I often feel you with me when we drive. I sense you sitting in the front passenger seat, looking out of the side window with your little hand resting on mine, on the floor shifter between us. It has always been a warm connection. It is how we used to drive together, and I have found it comforting these last months.

All of this now brings me back to yesterday. I had just had an intense grief session with Roz, and I was already overwhelmed by feelings of loss when I got back into my car and started back to work. And suddenly, I felt you there, with your hand on mine, and I became lost in our contact. Somehow, I managed to drive safely, but I found myself traveling east on 8 Mile Road instead of using the freeway. Now, 8 Mile Road is divided and has four lanes each way, so it's fast, but it does have traffic lights, so it is not as fast as the freeway, my usual choice. I can only credit this unaccustomed routing to my total distraction. We rode along in the far left lane, just you and I, and I didn't pay attention to the passing scenery, or much else, when, as often happens on 8 Mile Road, we had to stop at a red light.

And, at that moment, you left. I was totally surprised by the abruptness of your departure. There was no warning, no conversation. You just vanished. In a daze, I looked around for the first time, and I saw that the garage door company that had issued my opener was on my right, about 100 feet ahead. I was surprised. I had had no idea where it was located, much less here on 8 Mile Road. My mind was still reeling from all the intense feelings, but, sort of abstractly, I decided to try to go there to get an opener for Linda. I doubted that I could cross three lanes of traffic in time, but I thought I would at least try. If I couldn't make it this time, I would certainly know where to come back. You know, I still felt only partially connected to reality.

Somehow, though, when the light changed and no one next to me moved, I was not totally surprised. I was able easily to change lanes three times and to pull into the parking lot. I went into the building and asked for a new opener just like the one I brought into the store with me. A few minutes passed, and the owner came out to talk to me, and I went from daze to shock. I think that you knew who he was, didn't you? It was the driver whose truck hit you.

Until this moment, I had had no idea that he owned this company, nor where the company was located, and yet here I was, talking to the man who killed you. As if from a great distance, I heard him talk about his life since the accident. And you know what? He seemed to want me to feel sorry for him. His business is in difficulty, his wife is divorcing him and Mom is suing him. I listened to all this with the detachment of someone who is not sure he is awake. Then, I heard him ask how I was doing, and I heard my voice respond, as if underwater, that I was OK. What else could I have said under the circumstances? Still in a dreamlike state, I left. Later, I determined to change my garage door and all of the openers to another brand as soon as I could.

Andrew, it seems to me that you led me there. How else could I have found it? Coincidence? No way!

Well, whatever it was, it worked. I am getting angry again, angry at your death and at the pain in your life. I'm usually uncomfortable with anger, but I can see that I need it. Perhaps I'll get stuck again sometime, but for now, thanks to you, I can tell that I'm moving forward again.

Love,
Dad

May 19, 1989

Dear Andrew,

Today, it is one year since your death. On the one hand, sometimes it feels like an eternity since this date last year. There have been days that crawled past at a snail's pace, as I struggled with pain and disbelief. There have been hours that masqueraded as eons and minutes in which I was excruciatingly aware of each second. On the other hand, the accident often seems as though it happened a moment ago, and, lately, I have been seeing it over and over. I am haunted by the events of that day, nay the events of the weeks up to and including that day. And yet, there is still an aura of unreality to it all, as if it was a bad dream from which I will wake shortly, and we will have a good laugh.

It was just a year ago, and yet a few moments ago, when you and I were planning weekends together, planning projects, planning ... As I look back through the telescope of memory, I can transport myself off to that time in an instant, with its expectations and anxieties, and then, on May 19, time's abrupt ending. How do you commemorate an anniversary of the ending of time?

Yet I know that a year has gone by, because my memory can be refocused on more recent events, as if selecting from a catalog. I have too many changes in my life, too many new people, too many occurrences, all experienced in the now, to deny the passage of time. It is not merely that this has been a painful year that has slowed its passing, but distance also accumulates when counting significant events. And what determines significance? Well, my sensitivity has certainly increased since one year ago, and that has made everything that much more consequential.

There is another side to this, you know. For the better part of this last year, my habits are changed because of what happened twelve months ago. I used to be home from work by 5:30 p.m. every Tuesday and Thursday, to pick you up for the evening. I used to spend every other weekend with you. I used to help coach your baseball team in the spring and your soccer team in the fall. I used to commit large portions of my week to sharing with you. So it is more than just planning. Your death left an enormous empty space in my heart, yes, but also in my day. The sweet regularity of years was destroyed in a few moments, and, in the intervening year, without having consciously planned it, I have evolved a new routine that does not include you in the same way as before. That fact alone has played havoc with my sense of time since you died. It is also part of the special sadness that is this anniversary.

People have asked me how I will "get through" today. Some have even gone so far as to advise me, using that same phrase, how to "get through" the day. I see it differently. I felt the energy from the impending anniversary approach several weeks ago, and I made plans to spend the day with you, all day. And so I have, whether watching the Superman movie, as I did on your birthday, or visiting the cemetery, or reminiscing about you with friends. Writing to you has also been a way of sharing with you. All of these activities have been painful, it's true, but in my heart, I would have been with you in any case. You would have dominated my internal reality. I survived this year by being true to my inner self. Today was no exception. I'm not the same after the anniversary as before -- it is a form of "goodbye" and each one of those changes me in some, as yet, undefined way.

I want you to know that I have not felt alone today -- lots of my friends have remembered the date and either called or written. My family has also reached out to me.

My new friends from the bereavement support group have been there, as well. And you, of course, you have been here.

Love,
Dad

July 17, 1989

Dear Andrew,

I have never thought about buying a work of art before. After all, when I was growing up, I was used to walls filled with my Grandfather's paintings. So, who needs to buy art? But, now, I did. Why? Well, it involves a trip that Linda and I took up North a few weeks ago, and it ties into a trip that I took a long, long time ago, when I was just about the same age you would be today.

I don't think you have ever been to Glen Arbor, Michigan. During your life, I had not yet been there myself, so, I'll just tell you that Glen Arbor has a lot of craft stores and art outlets. One such store is called "The Glen Arbor City Limits". It usually displays a large variety of unusual and beautiful items, and Lin and I like to go there.

This particular trip, the store was showing, among other pieces, the work of a Native American artist named "A. Benally". I noticed that his paintings were scattered throughout the store, but I didn't stop to look closely. That is, I didn't think that I had stopped. Apparently, I was mistaken, because, suddenly, as if wakened from a sound sleep, I was aware that Linda was at my elbow and speaking to me.

Where had I been, she wanted to know. She thought that I had followed her out of the store, and she had gotten all the way to the next one when she discovered I wasn't there. She came back to find me transfixed, facing the Benally painting next to the doorway. It was called, "The Bear People". She looked at it and said, "I can see why you couldn't take your eyes off of it." The painting showed two Native Americans on horseback, riding into a blizzard. They are covered by bearskins in what appears to be a vain effort to keep warm. The surrounding landscape is bleak. Overhead, however, is the image of a large bear next to a ghostly moon, and it is clear that the bear spirit is watching over the tormented mortals below.

Usually, when we admire and appreciate a painting, it is as an observer. We are outside the work, relishing the color, the composition, the technique. Ideally, we may even be able to feel the emotion in the work, and to carry it with us in this way. I was not an observer to this painting. I was a participant. I was in the painting. I was one of the bear people, face to the driving cold, and the bear spirit was watching over me. And so, I have felt you, my Little Running Bear, as a vigilant protector these last months, sometimes observing, sometimes guiding. It was as though Benally painted this image with us in mind.

How much was the painting, I asked, and I found that it cost more than I could imagine spending. And so I didn't buy it. As much as it spoke to my soul, I left it in the store. But, for the rest of the trip, I was haunted by the memory of the bear spirit and his companion, the moon. Once home, my consciousness remained split between what was now before me, and the image I left behind.

Finally, after describing to others the effect on me of this amazing work of art, I thought that I might consider buying it after all. A quick call to The Glen Arbor City Limits confirmed that the painting had not been sold, and, yes, they would hold it for a few days while I came to a final decision. In the mean time, they would mail me some information about the artist that might help me to make up my mind.

The next day, I wondered, "What am I waiting for? After all, the painting affects me deeply. How often does that happen? Why not just get it?" With Linda's encouragement, I was resolved. I called The Glen Arbor City Limits and made arrangements for the purchase and delivery of "The Bear People". It was done. I could hardly wait! In the excitement and relief of the moment, I had forgotten that a postal packet was, even now, en route from Glen Arbor.

The next day, when the mail came, it included the letter from The City Limits. You know, sometimes, in life, events seem to conspire to coincide in a manner that would be considered unbelievable in a work of fiction. Indeed, in our language, in our culture, we have no words to describe the relationship inherent in a sequence of happenings when that series seems less than causal, but yet somewhat more than chance. Our faith in science and logic is so strong that we are not comfortable with the shadow land between simple cause and effect, on the one hand, and coincidence, on the other. This gray area, which, in our culture, defies explanation and eludes description, seems to be my province these days, and particularly on opening the letter from Glen Arbor.

First of all, the artist, A. Benally, goes by the name "Andrew", and thus is closed a small circle relating you and me to this painting. The emotional appeal inherent in the art itself had been extended to the artist. But there is a much larger circle, as well, that relates to a time over 30 years ago.

I was 10 years old, and my family had taken a train trip from our urban home in Washington, DC to the unaccustomed desert environs of Arizona. It was a heady trip, filled with new sights and impressions that etched themselves, as though with sand, into my susceptible memory. I was simply overwhelmed. However, notwithstanding the flood to my senses, I had one experience that dominated all the others in intensity. It was one of those events that refuses to remain obediently in the past, but instead lives forever on the edge of yesterday.

I remember, as I relive it yet again, our sojourn in the Navajo reservation that straddles Arizona and New Mexico, because there, I encountered the spirits of generations of Americans long past. They spoke to me then, and, sometimes, they speak to me yet.

The entrance to the reservation was unimposing—neither bridge nor gate served to forewarn callers of what lay ahead, and of what was left behind. And so I was unprepared. In particular, I was unprepared to behold the crumbling two-story house that, I was told, was the ruin of the home of the last chief of the Navajo. Yet, that was what lay before me. And, suddenly, it was as if the deteriorating walls spoke to me, and the sand around us, and finally, the wind. It was the same ghostly wind that I had heard and felt in my dream of the endless wall, shortly after your death. Lost in my senses, I knew the pain of the last chief, presiding over the end of his people, his culture. I knew the hopelessness, the sense of inevitability, the consciousness of the coming abyss. That is what the wind whispered, echoed by the rustling sand, and the moaning of the walls.

What I could not know then, was that an infant Navajo boy, who would be called Andrew, was born on that reservation at just about that time, and that he would grow up to paint pictures in an effort to rebuild Navajo culture. He would grow up to paint "The Bear People". In Benally's own words, "I describe my work as a form of mysticism, or what you would call 'vision paintings'. They focus on the Indian's belief between the spirit and man." And so they do. This was the information contained in the mailing from Glen Arbor. And thus closed another circle, spanning over 30 years and over 3,000 miles.

Today, "The Bear People" hangs in our dining room, alongside your shield and one of your own paintings. It is your wall in our house.

Love,
Dad

November 4, 1989

Dear Andrew,

On October 15, Linda and I were married. The day was incredibly beautiful, with temperatures over 80 degrees and brilliant sunshine. It was the kind of late fall day that comes occasionally in Michigan, that is both a momentary pause in the inevitable slide into cold and gray and a wistful reminder of summer days past.

The wedding itself was all I could have wished. Linda was a beautiful bride, and I love her so much. I went through a full range of emotions, as you can imagine -- tears of joy and tears of sorrow. I did not feel you there, although we remembered you, as we remembered my father and Lin's father, and we wished all of you could have been present. I thought of you often through the ceremony and the reception, and I wondered what you would have made of it all. Perhaps it would have been a difficult day for you. I suppose it would have depended on your relationship with Lin and I can only hope that you would have liked her.

The day after the wedding, we left on our honeymoon, and what a trip it was! We flew to Hawaii, to the big island, and we spent a week there. What an amazing place! One side of the island, where we stayed, is covered with hardened, black lava and, except for the color, it resembles nothing so much as the surface of the moon. This side is virtually arid. By contrast, the other side is lush with vegetation because of the heavy rainfall. This other side also presents picturesque rock cliffs along the shoreline of the Pacific Ocean. On the one hand, it is more beautiful, but it is also the side that is subject to tidal waves. There is the Banyan tree, whose branches grow down into the ground, where they root and emerge as a new tree some distance from the original. It's possible to have a whole forest of Banyan trees that, in fact, consists of one tree. We took a helicopter ride and flew into a live volcano, and watched molten lava flow into the ocean. We took a submarine trip and saw fish feeding in their natural habitat, 100 feet below the surface. We saw enormous manta rays, gliding like underwater shadows near the shore, feeding on the plankton along the bottom. What an amazing adventure!

And now we are home, getting back into our lives of work, leisure and everyday companionship. But, part of our everyday life is a not so everyday decision. We are deciding whether or not we will have a baby, and I wanted to tell you about it.

Shortly after you were killed, I heard a suggestion for dealing with my grief. The idea was to have another child as soon as possible as a means of coping with the loss. I don't want to say that this is a bad idea, but I remember thinking, at the time, that I certainly would not be able to do it. In fact, I knew the instant I heard the idea that it would not help me, even if I had been in a position to start a new family at the time.

You see, for me, it would have been impossible, so soon after your death, to separate the new baby from you. Unconsciously, and perhaps even consciously, I would have expected the infant to be a replacement for you -- an impossible situation, both for me and for the baby. So, the question remains, is now still too soon for me? That is, at this time, would a new baby still seem to me like a replacement for you in my heart and in my life?

Do you see the danger? If I embark on this new venture, if I follow the course of family with Linda, and, at the same time, I am looking to substitute a new baby for the little boy I lost in you, then there will be all sorts of negative consequences, the least of which is that I may abort my own grief process and delay healing. Even more seriously, the baby, who is likely to be quite different from you, would, at minimum, have a difficult childhood (and adulthood!) because of the inescapable pressure to live up to the expectation that he or she "should" really "be" someone else.

Yet, don't we parents frequently make this kind of mistake with a newborn, even when we have not previously suffered the loss of a child? How often does a couple, on contemplating starting a family or just adding to an existing family, go through a self-examination to determine "who" a new child is preconceived to "be"? Not very often, in my experience. Perhaps, in fact, most children are born into an ocean of expectation, and, to find their true selves, they must find an inland waterway along which they must swim upstream against the current of their parents' beliefs. I have no interest in passing that kind of legacy on to a new child.

No matter my intent, isn't this just the peril I court if I start a new family? Wouldn't the temptation be enormous, almost undeniable, to mold a new child into a copy of you? This is the question I must answer. This is what I must settle beyond a doubt: if Lin and I have a baby, I feel that child must come into the world a beloved stranger, eager to know and to become known, free of preconceived notions. I have no concern about Linda, only about myself.

Oh, Andrew, the other part of this decision is about my fear, my vulnerability. It seems I must know not only my own mind, but also my own heart. The death of a child is the worst thing that can happen to a parent. Your death hurt me profoundly, and it continues to hurt. Can I dare to cherish another child the way I cherished you and Leah? Can I live with life's uncertainty, which I have seen only too clearly? Until August 1988, and Walden, I didn't know that I could ever love again. Now I know that I can. Perhaps, given who I am, I have to. And I do. Would it happen again? Would I allow it to? Can I know without trying?

I have lived with all these questions for a while now, and I will continue to live with them for a few more months before we make a decision, but I can already feel the direction in which I am being pulled, even if slightly upstream, by my own nature. I have always loved being Leah's father, and I have always loved being yours.

Thanks for listening.

Love,

Dad

January 1, 1990

Dear Andrew,

Last night, Lin and I went to see the musical group, Manhattan Transfer, with Dale and Pam, to celebrate New Years Eve. The music was wonderful. I found myself tapping my foot in time and simultaneously, tears were streaming down my cheeks. You see, it is the first day of the new year, and a new decade. You were born at the end of the decade of the seventies, and lived nearly all of the decade of the eighties. The nineties is the first new decade without you. I have noticed that more and more, my experiences are amalgams of what seem to be intensely opposite feelings. So it was last night, with the joy of the music and the company, alongside the recognition of one more demarcation of time passing without you. New Year's Eve is often a time of reflection and hope for the future, for a happy new year. I can still barely comprehend what is past, much less guess what is to be.

I have felt a change in me over the last year. I think that it has happened slowly and I am only now beginning to be aware of it. The reality of your loss has been sinking in, and the pain, while less raw, has gone deep into my soul. Sometimes, I think that it is too deep for words, and I am frustrated at my inability to explain. I listen to myself and I am dismayed at how little of my internal reality my phrases express. In addition, I am not even sure whether I grieve more for my loss or for yours. I cannot distinguish anymore. The pain is so general and nonspecific.

There is a core of loss and grief that seems to concentrate in the center of my being, where the "I" is located, and every thought, every idea, every perception must pass it by en route to my consciousness. In the process, then, a piece of the sadness, like a weight, is added onto the traveler and all that I see, all that I know and all that I feel are a part of the pain, and, in turn, partake of the pain. And so there is a heaviness that is a companion to all I am and all I do.

This phase -- I hope it is a phase -- is truly isolating, in spite of the fact that I have willing listeners all around. How can I tell them what I feel when I am ultimately unsatisfied with speaking? Yet, if I don't try, don't they then rightly assume that I am fine? Worse, when I try to answer even the sincere, "How are you doing?", my tears dry up. How easily my feelings disappear into hiding under a barrage of words! My ability to express my inner status has always helped me to make the personal connections that have so nurtured me, and now I feel robbed of my verbal strengths.

The pain often seems to have gone too deep even for tears. It is residing in some reservoir that has no direct contact with tear ducts, and so I am denied even this most primitive expression. I think it would be easier to be angry, almost a relief, because anger is so close to the surface and so straightforward to reveal. Nevertheless, in spite of all that I feel, or perhaps because of it, I am determined to live.

Lately, the accident seems so immediate, and I feel the need to process it. Still, I have been generally unable to tell people what I saw, but, now, I think that I'm getting near to being able to write it. How? I'm not yet sure.

On Christmas Eve, Alex and I went to the cemetery. I had been feeling the need to give you something. After all, I very much still feel myself to be your father. Yet, what can I give? What can I give to any child? Things are nice, but somehow not satisfactory. I have come to understand that the only gift I have to offer that has any meaning is my love. But, as a symbol of that, I wanted to leave you something at the grave. You always loved to collect odds and ends that could be used in some future construction project, and so I brought a few of your old batteries, and nails and screws to put on the ground. Also, I wanted to leave a message but I couldn't find the words. So, I allowed myself to drift to a place where I could just talk to you and I knew then what I wanted to say:

"Dear Andrew,
I wish you:
Kites and bats and shoes with cleats;
Model trains and cars and running free;
Bows and arrows and basketballs;
Drawing pencils and paper, treasure hunts;
Popcorn with your favorite movies;
Waffles for breakfast, ice cream for dessert;
And if dreams there be,
Then dreams come true.
All this and more, I wish for you.
I love you always.
Dad"

The cemetery was cold and bleak. A number of the stone monuments had been toppled. We brushed the snow off of your grave marker and I felt a deep sadness come over me as I read, "Andrew B. Goor, born September 19, 1979, died May 19, 1988". I nailed down the note and covered it with snow. Then, I uncovered it again, buried the batteries and stood up. I felt you rush up to me and give me a big hug around the waist. Then, in a flash, you were gone again. Alex and I walked slowly around the cemetery in the bitter wind. Overhead, three black birds slowly and somberly landed in a bare tree. I felt that we were not alone.

I miss you.
Love,
Dad

January 7, 1990

Dear Andrew,

It's late, and grows later every moment. All this time, I have been unable to tell you or anyone else what happened the day you died. Time is frozen on that day. And now, for some reason, now, I am ready to tell you, to tell the world, what happened to you. Now, I need to. I'm sorry. It was horrible that day, and it will be horrible to read. And, yet, as I write this, I am back there -- it is May, 1988 and I see it all again. It has been thousands of times. Now it will be one more.

Oh, my son! How can I write to you? What can I say? You're dead. That is so hard for me for me to say or write. Sometimes, that is all I can think of, over and over: you're dead; *you're dead*; *you're dead*! And yet, sometimes that is so hard for me to believe. And it wasn't an accident. No, it couldn't be. At least, not to me. To me, it feels as though you were murdered. I want to scream, "Bloody murder!" at the top of my lungs so that everyone can hear. I want everyone to know what happened. And there does not seem to be a forum for truth, except as I write it, except as I scream it.

It was Thursday in May and I had been having a good day -- well, not a good day, really, but a great day. I had had a breakthrough at work and suddenly, after months of being stymied, my research was going exceptionally well. I was making progress again. I felt good. I felt good about us. No matter what happened at court, no matter what anyone else did, you and I would continue to be close. I was being the father I wanted to be, and nothing could get in the way of that. I felt at peace.

Rain was hanging in the air as I drove to Mom's house to pick you up. I knew that you would be excited about the plans I had. Today, we would eat a quick dinner and go to the batting cage where a machine would pitch balls to you and you could take batting practice. Neither of us had ever been there, although we had talked about it. I was anxious to see you. I was looking forward to being with you. It seemed an age before I found myself driving up Adams and making a left onto Abbey.

I saw you immediately. You and Nate were on the sidewalk in front of Mom's house and you were on Nate's bright yellow wagon. You were facing me, and you seemed to recognize my car as I turned. You got off of the wagon and stood on your tiptoes, as if to see me better, and you smiled. And then you did something really unusual. You raised your arm as high as it would go and you waved. It was not a small, surreptitious wave, but a great, big greeting. You had never done that.

You never showed any affection toward me at all at Mom's house. You always waited until after you were in the car and we were on the way, perhaps even around the corner, safe. And then you would give me a hug, or pat my hand on the gearshift, as you said "hi". (Sometimes, I can still feel your hugs, and every now and then, I am aware of your little hand softly touching mine on the gearshift.) And so it was really remarkable to me that you waved, right there on the sidewalk in front of Mom's, in full view of the whole neighborhood, and right in front of Nate. At the time, it felt warm and loving.

As I pulled into Mom's driveway and got out of the car, you went with Nate to his driveway. I had a brief moment to reflect on how things had changed. It used to be such a struggle for me when I came to pick you up. The events of the divorce, and the effect on you and on Leah, all had upset me, and I fought to stay in touch with you, to be a father to you, to live up to the separation agreement, and, yes, I fought to avoid feeling controlled. Today, I didn't feel threatened by anything. Today was different. I was relaxed. I could handle anything.

Then, through the hedge, I could see you on the wagon, accelerating rapidly down Nate's driveway. I couldn't see what, or who, was accelerating you, only that you were on the wagon and moving fast. In an instant, you were past the hedge and across the sidewalk. I could see you clearly now. I saw that you were kneeling on the wagon, and that you were going into the street. At the same time, I saw a black truck in the distance down Abbey, back by Poppleton Street, and it was headed your way!

Then everything went into slow motion. Your head was high, erect. I could see that your neck was extended and that you were focusing on the opposite side of the street. In your concentration, you didn't move. You seemed so small as the wagon rolled toward the center of the street.

As I relive it, a voice in my head screams frantically, "OH, MY GOD, ANDREW! DO SOMETHING! OH, MY GOD! MY SON IS GOING TO BE HIT! THERE IS NOTHING I CAN DO! WHAT CAN I DO?" But, as I remember it, that was not how it was on that day. No, as the wagon entered the street, my world went utterly silent, outside and inside. It was as though all words stopped, and so I don't know how to describe it in words. But, I knew what was about to happen. I seemed to just know, without language, without pictures. What was all beyond words, beyond conceiving, was happening. Soundlessly, slowly, agonizingly, the wagon rolled on, and I watched. And there were just the two of us: you, helplessly on the wagon, and me, helplessly watching.

As the wagon approached the raised center of the street, it slowed almost to a standstill. There was never a doubt in my mind but that it had enough momentum to continue over to the other side. And still, you never moved. You just stared straight ahead, neither to left or right, just straight. You seemed so vulnerable. It seemed that the wagon paused forever at the center of the street. And the truck just got bigger and bigger, never slowing, never swerving. It just came on and on. And you started down the other side, as my horror grew. And the truck kept coming. But now you were accelerating toward the far side of the street. You were going faster. I began to think, to *hope*, that *maybe*, you might make it all the way across. OH, GOD, *PLEASE*!

With the front wheels of the wagon almost to the grass, the right front wheel of the truck hit the wagon. Another six inches and you would have been clear. Still apparently in slow motion, you were thrown backwards into the air, into a standing posture and you were twisted a half turn, to face the truck, and then, time returned to normal. In an instant, you were pulled by your feet under first the front wheel and then the rear wheel. Finally, the driver of the truck hit the brakes, there was the screech of rubber on pavement and the truck stopped, and all was still. Once again, all was silent.

I went running up to you, and I immediately knew that you were dead. Your brains were spilled out in a long line onto the street. They were bright red and braided in texture, with blood trailing off down the pavement, toward the grass and the safety that was not to be. *I can never forget.* The skin on your leg was worn down to white bone, and yet there was no bleeding. Your forehead was crushed and your eye sockets did not seem to have room for your eyes. Your face was pale. Your lips were red, but you had no expression. Your hands lay by your side, oh so still and limp. One of your shoes had been torn off and was lying in the street. It started to rain lightly, gently, and sounds returned, softly at first.

Then, I turned and ran to Mom's door and I pounded on the door through the screen, tearing the screen. I screamed, "ANDREW'S BEEN HIT BY A CAR! CALL AN AMBULANCE!" Then, I came back to be with you. I picked up your shoe and held it to me. I clutched it to me and I wouldn't part with it until I was at home, much later. When I turned from you again, I saw the truck and I screamed as loud as I could, and I hit the truck with my fist, once. *FUCKIN' TRUCK!*

Mom came out now and ran up to your body and put her head on your stomach. She called out, "I love you, Andrew!" I reached out to her and she said, angrily, "Don't you *touch* me!" Leah came out, screaming, "IT CAN'T BE TRUE! IT *CAN'T* BE TRUE!" and I held her, until Mom took her away, saying, "Come to your Mother who loves you."

The rest consists of disconnected memories. Mom tried to make Leah look at your mangled body, claiming it would be easier for her later, but Leah managed to escape her. Then, Leah went inside, taking me with her. She called someone on the phone and handed it to me. A voice on the other end, as if from a great distance, told me that this was all my fault, and I simply dropped the phone and walked away. I can't believe that you're dead, and I can't believe that people are acting like this. Somehow, I called Roz and I called some friends and I waited for them to pick me up.

I went back outside to be with you, but the emergency team asked me to move away. I remember crying on the shoulders of some of the neighbors I knew, when Nate's father came up to me. He slapped me on the back, and said, "Well, tough luck, old buddy." I just can't believe how he said it, so casually, as if I had just lost a bridge hand, instead of my son. I hate that man.

I was in a daze, so I don't remember much more. Somehow, I was taken into Mom's house where I cried on Grandma Dora's shoulder and on Joyce Dean's shoulder. Mom was talking rapidly about who should be called and what should be done. She spoke in an even tone, with no feeling, perhaps trying desperately to control feeling. I remember Grandma saying to her, "It would be better if you could cry." But Mom couldn't. I heard her say, over and over, "I don't understand life. First the divorce, and now this."

After a while, I needed quiet, and I went outside on the front porch to wait for my friends to pick me up. It was drizzling. I saw the "rescue" team wheel away your body on a gurney like so much meat. They had covered you all up with a sheet. But one arm dangled uncovered over the edge of the cart. They wheeled your body into the ambulance. It was the last I ever saw of you. I felt so heavy inside, so hopeless, so dead. Suddenly, without warning, the earth had opened up, and, as I watched, it had swallowed you and then, in an instant, closed again. Everything looked so bleak and colorless.

The next thing I knew, I was home and friends were around, loving friends. There were no more of the incredible cruelties I felt near Mom's house. But the fact of your death came with me. I kept seeing the accident over and over, your face, your brains, over and over and over. Roz and Fred came to my house and lit a large candle that continued to burn for many days. Fred held me on his lap as I sobbed, much as I used to hold you in the past.

Eventually, I was hungry, and I knew that I could not eat meat, not after what I had seen. I have not eaten meat since. I don't know if I ever will. Even the thought of raw meat, much less the sight of it, takes me back to the sight of your brains, your blood, your bones. And I can't separate cooked meat from the raw meat that it was, or the live animal that it was, or the very live little boy that you were.

Bedtime was horrible. I was terrified that your pale and mutilated face would enter my dreams, or worse, that I would see you like that when I was awake in the night. Visions of your death, of the wagon, the truck, continued over and over again. As soon as my mind reenacted the scene to completion, it started again, and again.

In the days that followed, my friends surrounded me with love and support, and they helped me to be able to learn to function again. It was several weeks before I could drive again, and begin to go back to work. I remember that, at first, I could do nothing at work but sit in my office and stare. Nothing seemed important. Nothing felt the same as before. I felt like a stranger in my own world. I was only beginning to be able to accept that you had really been killed, that you are dead. At that time, I was in no condition to deal with the circumstances of your death, and of your life leading up to your death. But that has changed as I have grown.

Somehow, one day at a time, I have made it from the excruciating moment of your death, on that dreadful day, to now, a relatively tranquil time. But, lately, I become agitated when I think about the circumstances of your death, and of your life. No, agitated isn't the word. There are so many pieces, and sometimes they fit together one way, sometimes another and sometimes not at all. I'm confused and I'm enraged! There are so many people I could blame, so many I do blame. That's why your death feels like murder. How do I prove my case? How do I unravel the tangled facts of your life now that you're dead, when it was so difficult before? I guess it will take time, and now, suddenly, I'm tired.

I love you so very much, and I miss you.

Love,

Dad

January 16, 1990

Dear Andrew,

I feel battered by such extremes of feeling. I alternate between rage and sadness, bordering on depression. I know that your death was not a pure accident. It cannot be. There are so many reasons. I see so many layers of neglect and carelessness, starting with a legal system that did not see you, and ending with a driver who I am certain did not see you.

Sometimes, suddenly, I am so angry, and I don't know how to talk about or how to write about it. I see the picture so clearly, and when I try to express it, I lose it all. The magnitude of this is so huge, and the web so intricate, what I know is so horrible and so maddening. I feel as though you were murdered. Yes, murdered! How could it be less? I feel so much rage! And I can line up the accused, and, at least in my mind, I can charge them with their crimes. For each of them is guilty of hurting you, of helping to put you in the street in front of that car, as it hurtled irresistibly down the street toward us both, and then ended your life, and changed mine forever.

And the fire of my outrage leaves no shadow of a doubt, no corner of truth unlit. All of my uncertainty during the divorce, in those dark days before your final ride, I have replaced with the certainty of hindsight. These were no innocent bystanders that I name. No, they all contributed to your precarious and ultimately fatal position. These were significant people in your life, people of trust and responsibility, family and non-family. Shall I name them here? What's the point? You know who they are.

Oh, how I want them to know what they did. I just want them to feel the pain that I feel, and to know that they are at least partly responsible. And how can I do that? I don't know, but I need to have the truth told. I need people to know so that I am not alone with it. I need to tell the truth. And I know the truth, which is that a number of people are to blame for what happened to you. Oh, yes, this one lied, and that one betrayed your trust, and another one ignored the seriousness of what was happening to you, and another one directly put you in danger. Each one whittled away a chink in your security. Each one put you closer to the edge of danger.

Oh, Andrew! I want them to know anguish, as I do. I want them to know loss, as I do. I want them to know guilt, and to punish themselves. Yet, I know that they don't believe, even for a moment, that your death was anything other than a tragic accident. I am obsessed with showing them -- I have a list of those who were responsible, and I understand how all the strands of events wove the final fabric of your death. I see it all, just so clearly, and agonizingly. I am in torment until I can expose what I know.

And yet, how will they know? How could they know? They did not see you as I did. They did not share with you, as I did. They did not know, and love, the complex little boy you were, torn and struggling between two worlds, perhaps neither of your choosing. They did not have the kind of deep connection with you that speaks of minds and hearts and souls, and that often took my breath away. They did not have all of these things, so how could they know my loss? They were on the outside, looking in and seeing only what they wanted to see.

How could they know? Even before you died, they were so sure of what they knew, so sure of their actions, so sure of their rights and wrongs. How do I crack through that kind of armor? All through the divorce, I agonized over every decision. I knew only that I wanted to do what was best for you and for Leah, but I was never quite sure what that might be. Our situation was so complicated, so difficult. How could anyone be sure of what was right? How could anyone be totally free of doubt? And yet it seemed that so many people in our lives, people we both knew, were untroubled and unconflicted. They were so sure of their world view, and they could not be persuaded of the danger to you. They are among the ones that are to blame for your death. But, they will not know. If I could not persuade them before, they will not now open their sight. If I could write them as characters in a play, to be true to what I know of them, I would have to maintain their consistency. Without exception, they would deny my claims and refute my observations. Even my fictitious characters would deny responsibility. Your death has only increased their investment in their one-sided views. Mightn't they, in fact, even blame me?

But, this feels so hollow, so empty to me -- that they get to live their lives with no shadow of guilt or regret, and somehow I must carry your story, with all of its pain, ambiguity and uncertainty, inside myself, alone. It is too much! How do I live with this rage? It seems that the world at large preaches forgiveness. How can I come to forgive someone who feels no guilt, and who admits none? And how do I live in a world where your death is seen as an accident, and nothing more?

Rage! Around in my head go all of these thoughts, mixed with the scene of you in the street, and what I view as atrocities from your life. And when it has reached a fever pitch, I can sustain it no longer, much as I would like to stay in this angry state. It is almost comfortable for me there. At least it is tolerable. But, I can't hang on. It takes too much energy, so still thinking of the list of the guilty, I cool down, and the shadows return. I lapse into thoughts of "what does it matter?" After all, the end is the same -- you were killed on May 19, 1988. What does it matter what happened before? That date has become a pivot point in my life. There is all that came before, and all that has come after. Doubts and "reasonable" hypotheses begin again. And I am plunged into a sea of sadness and loss, but not for long. Soon I am thrown up onto the rocky shore of my memory, drenched in my feelings of helplessness, furious anew at a hundred outrageous and indifferent acts, and remembering my utter frustration as your advocate. I can see them individually and as a whole, and I know they added up. I remember with such clarity. And yet, my doubts remain. As bad as things were before you died, what actually caused your death? And, at this moment, I have no answer to that question. Perhaps at another moment ...

But, I am wracked by my need to know and to put to rest my fundamental doubts. For this, it seems, is my most important unanswered question. Why were you in the street that day, and why didn't the driver see you? Sometimes I'm so sure that I know. And sometimes I know that I will never really know the truth. Damn it, Andrew! There must have been a reason! There must have been causes! I understand so much, and I want to know. I need to know! Why will I never know?

Love,
Dad

April 22, 1990

Dear Andrew,

A few days ago, I observed the 23rd month "anniversary" of your death. It was even on a Thursday. We are coming up on the second year since you were killed. Sometimes, I simply can't believe that it has been so long. It still seems like yesterday to me, and yet it also feels like forever ago, as though it happened at the beginning of my life. About so many things now, I feel mixed up in time, as if I have completely lost my sense of time. Linear time has no meaning to me anymore.

A few days ago, I had a dream about you. I dreamt that I knew exactly what was going to happen, that Nate would push you into the street and the same driver would hit you and kill you. I warned you about it, and I was prepared when I arrived to pick you up. I realized, as I was pulling into the driveway, that everyone knew what was about to happen. As soon as I got out of the car, I ran to Nate's driveway and stopped you from going into the street. But the driver reacted differently than he did in actuality. He slammed on his brakes. His truck went out of control and spun around, and you were hit anyway. It happened differently, but you were killed just the same. However, I don't understand. Why were you playing with Nate when you, and Mom, both knew what would happen? Why did Nate push you into the street when he knew what would happen? Only the driver and I changed what we did to try to prevent your death. I don't know how to make sense of this, and I was aware of my confusion as part of the dream. What did the other people in the dream have in mind? Maybe it doesn't matter. After all, I still feel that you were cheated out of your whole life.

Then, I awoke and I saw you, or rather felt you, standing there beside the bed, looking down at me as if you were fresh from the dream. It was a momentary feeling, and then you were gone. There was no particular mood to your visit. I simply felt you there. And I am here.

Love,
Dad

May 12, 1990

Dear Andrew,

In one week, it will be two years since you were killed. It has seemed a lifetime to me. A lot has happened since you died. My life has changed so much that I find it hard to comprehend. Right now, I feel that I live on a vertex connecting past and future. There have been so many endings, and, now, so many new beginnings. Linda and I have been married for seven months, and we are expecting a baby. Yes, we are going to have a little girl in October! I am excited and pleased, but I have so many other feelings, too. Where can I start?

When you and Leah were born, I thought that, because of my experience and understanding, I could keep you from feeling pain, especially the kind of pain that I felt in growing up. Oh, yes! It was going to be different for you. I wouldn't abandon you at night if you were frightened. I wouldn't push you to do things you didn't want to do. I wouldn't pressure you about school. On and on my list went. I didn't realize how many ways I was wrong.

I didn't realize that pain can also be a part of growth, or that growth even requires a kind of pain. I didn't want to know how it hurts to say goodbye, and that going on to something new is mixed joy and sorrow. I didn't know that my wisdom came as much from my failures as from my successes, and so I wanted to protect you from failure. I didn't know that my pain was unique to me and to my childhood, and that you would have to have your own experience. I didn't want to know that I couldn't protect you from loss, or from death.

In my own way, I have grown, and I know that, while I have a lot to give, there are some things beyond my control. Someday, I will either lose my new daughter, or she will lose me. Someday, I will either lose Leah, or she will lose me. There is nothing I can do about that, and it hurts to my very core. All during the divorce, I fought, not only to avoid losing you, but to keep you from losing me. And then you were killed.

And now, what frightens me the most is that I might abandon you. In my joy, in my love for my new daughter, I am so afraid that I might not be there for you. I'm afraid that I will forget to think about you, and that it will feel all right that you're not here. I'm afraid that I'll lose that warm spot in my heart where you live, in pain and sorrow, yes, but also with love and tenderness. Andrew, my new baby daughter will be alive. She'll cry and laugh and coo. She'll call me "Daddy" in her own magical way, and she'll wrap me around her little finger, just the way you and Leah did. But, she'll be here, and you won't. How I wish you could be here! I don't know what you'd think of your baby sister. Perhaps you'd love her. Perhaps you'd be jealous, or both. But, you're not here, and I'll never know for sure.

Andrew, I will have to change your room for the baby. I haven't wanted to do that yet. It still hurts so much when my new nephews play with your toys and sleep in your bed. If you were alive, I'm sure that we would find another way to use our space. If only … But changing your room feels to me like the first step in forgetting you, and I am not at all at peace with it. Already, your pictures feel two dimensional and static, and not at all like the very active and physical little boy you were. What used to remind me of you so tangibly is changing, and it's being replaced by something deeper and hard to explain. And I'm afraid of what is to be.

I am making a new life, Andrew. I have a new wife, and we have a new baby on the way. The work I did on robots for your entire life is winding down. I am thinking about new directions, about a new career. What? Where? With all my changes, I am so afraid that you won't be part of it, that you *can't* be a part of it. I feel myself moving on in my life.

Do you remember, Andrew, how you invented a "secret laboratory"? It could fly, and go into space and under water. It was a perfect fortress, and in it, you fantasized, you would take me along with a few friends, and we could go anywhere and do anything, and we were safe. I remember that, sometimes we would travel with a group, like the Cub Scouts, and we would listen to a speaker, who, responding to a question from the audience, might say, "Nothing can do *that*." That was your cue. You would catch my eye and wink. "Of course," you'd say later, "you knew that the secret laboratory could do *that*!" And I always said that, of course, I knew. I think I even believed in the secret laboratory myself, a little. You didn't know it, but I had saved a large carton so, if you wished, you could build a prototype version of the secret laboratory. I thought I could make you safe. In any case, I certainly tried.

Well, Andrew, the truth is that there is no secret laboratory. There is no safe place, no place where everything is possible. Where there is life, there is change, and there is risk. And I'm afraid. I love you.

Love,
Dad

May 17, 1990

Dear Andrew,

The dream I told you about, and my exhausting dreams every night, as the time approaches to mark the second year since you were killed, tell me of a piece of your death I have not yet worked out. I don't know for sure what it is. It's as though my fear of abandoning you now is a surrogate for some deep feeling that I abandoned you two years ago, and that somehow, I let you die.

As I let myself think of this, I see images of you on the wagon, rolling into the street, and I am frozen with fear. I cannot move. After you died, I had nightmares, recurrent dreams that I tried to run and catch the wagon before it rolled into the path of the on-coming truck. Every time I failed and you were killed. Finally, in my dream, I stopped the wagon, and you were already dead. What does that mean? Does it mean that I resolved that I could not have gotten there in time, or that it didn't matter what I did? I don't know.

But in those dreams, I never ran into the path of the on-coming truck. What would have happened if I had run in front of the truck to try to push you and the wagon to safety? Could I have gotten there fast enough? I would have had more time to get to you, but I would have been in danger of being killed myself. As I write this, I don't know the answers to those questions. I don't know if I was capable of risking death in that way for you. Why didn't I just react to try to save you? Would I have died to save you? Would I have died trying? Why am I alive when you are dead? I don't know. I just don't know. I feel ashamed. A father's job is to protect his children, no matter what. I feel that I let you down … in so many ways.

Last night I dreamt that Linda, my mother and I were listening to music on the radio and taping it. There was a kluge of wires between the radio and the tape machine that, somehow, also connected to the telephone answering machine. Suddenly, Leah's voice came on through the answering machine, happy and excited, inviting me to Mom's house for a birthday celebration on the 19th. "All of the J's would be there", she said. Yet, it was going to be the anniversary of your death. There would be no birthdays. I was so confused! Then, it seemed to me that she hung up and your voice came on, pleading, "Please, Dad, come home! Come home, Dad!" We were all shocked, and my mother and Lin began to talk about spirituality, and about prayers coming true, while I tried vainly to rewind the tape. I felt that it must be an old tape and that it was playing, not recording. When I awoke, I felt keenly how much you must have wanted me to get back together with Mom.

I'm sorry, Andrew. It could not be.

Love,

Dad

June 11, 1990

Dear Andrew,

I remember. It was the morning after you were killed. I slept fitfully, dreaming of your death over and over, all night. As I lay in bed, I heard the birds singing, and it all seemed so unreal. How can you be dead? How can the birds sing? And then I heard a sound so familiar that I had never really noticed it before. But this morning, it was a sound so brutal and invasive that it shocked me to wakefulness. It was your school bus going past my house, and I knew that you wouldn't be on it. You would never be on it again.

I felt dislocated, not so much out of body, but out of world. How can people be going to work, to school? How can there be traffic on Woodward Avenue? How can life be going on? It made me furious to think that the world was going about its business, as if this was any ordinary Friday. How could this be? You were dead, and the world would never be the same. I would never be the same. Every time I thought about your death, about what that means for you and for me, I was overwhelmed with pain so profound that I could not even begin to grasp it all. And how could I not think about it?

My bed was not a refuge. There was no hiding from the horror of the day, of every day. Showering, shaving, making breakfast all seemed pointless, empty tasks.

And then, you appeared to me. Your full round cheeks were wet, your eyes were compressed to slits and tears poured down your face. Your whole being seemed dissolved in pain and confusion. You were walking toward me, reaching out. You were my little boy, hurt and scared. "What happened to me, Dad? What happened?" you said.

I stared at you, and the pain rose in me like a wave from the pit of my stomach. "Oh my God!" I thought, "I can't tell him! I can't face this!"

And I shook my head violently, as, in my mind, I screamed, "NO!" I couldn't tell you. I just couldn't. But, my God, you were so real, as if I could just reach out and touch you, and yet I knew that I would never be able to touch you again. People around me asked what was the matter, and I said that I was still visualizing the accident. I couldn't tell anyone what I was seeing. And you kept coming back that day, sometimes in quiet moments, sometimes when there were people around, and I couldn't tell you. I couldn't speak the words, not even in my mind. And, yes, I did still see the accident over and over in my head. But I couldn't talk about that yet, either.

Dale was with me almost constantly that day. We both felt incredible clarity around what was important. I don't know how to describe the feeling. It was as though there had been an intense emotional starburst and, suddenly, there were no shadows. All was either light or dark. Whatever we felt, we shared. How we appeared to others was unimportant. Being true to ourselves was everything. I can't remember much about making the funeral arrangements. It all felt so horribly irrelevant somehow. And you kept appearing to me. "What happened, Dad?" And you and the wagon kept rolling into the street, over and over.

Mom invited me over to her house that afternoon. She had apologized for her anger at me at the time of the accident, and now she wanted me to be with her. I felt uncomfortable about being there alone, so Dale went with me. He remained in view the whole time I was there, an island of reality in what was now an unfamiliar world for me. Mom had called the newspapers and asked that they bring a photographer. She was holding interviews, telling her story. She asked me to sit with her on your bed while a reporter took her picture holding your cello. Her face was so drawn, so strained, but I never saw her cry. I refused to be in the picture, and they took it without me. I was astonished that she chose to do this. The reporter asked me how it felt for me to watch you being killed, and I responded angrily, and said that I wouldn't talk about it, and he mustn't print anything about it. At the time, my grief was not for public consumption, at least not in that form. But my tears were always near.

And then, "What happened, Dad?", and the wagon ...

My friends began to come to my house to be with me, to share their recollections of you and of us. They came to hug, to cry together, to share our sense of helplessness, of loss. In the midst of all this love, I missed you, and yet, somehow, I felt you there with us.

Later, Dale and I went back to Mom's house for a little while. Mom and I hugged and talked, but I felt out of place in her house. I used to live there, but now I felt like an alien. Was it all the changes I had made to myself since I moved out? Was it Mom's way of dealing with her feelings by talking rapidly in a monotone? She felt like a total stranger to me. Was this the woman I had lived with for over 17 years? In the meantime, Mom was talking and wouldn't be interrupted. My feelings seemed to be draining through my feet and into the floor. I had to get out of there. Then, I realized that I didn't feel you there. I felt you at my house, and I had to go back. More friends were waiting, with warmth and patience.

And then, "What happened, Dad?", and the wagon ...

The memories, the pain, all came in spasms. We sang songs that you and I liked to sing, and we laughed. But, when we sang, "Dragons live forever, but not so little boys", we all cried, and Puff the Magic Dragon took on new meaning for me. At bedtime, I was exhausted, and frightened. What would I see in the night? What would I dream? I would survive, I knew, because my friends would be there, sharing with me whatever I had to share. Some of them stayed through the night. They saw to it that I was never alone until I was ready.

And I did dream. I dreamt of the wagon going into the street, and then I was running, as hard as I knew how to run, and I dove, but I was too late. I couldn't catch you. And then, again ... And I awoke to a world without you in it, and I wished I were still asleep. In that twilight between sleep and wakefulness, I could feel you with me, and I hated to get up.

And when I did arise ... "What happened, Dad?", and the wagon ...

Then, more meaningless acts, showering, shaving, eating. I never felt hungry, but I ate anyway. What was important were the waves of feeling washing over me, and events became a blur. One moment, I felt loved and loving, another, sad, and another, angry, and yet another, astonishingly, amused. Most often, I felt that I had no future to look forward to and virtually no past before your death. I had only the present, and the moment you were killed.

Saturday afternoon, perhaps because of your love for kites, or perhaps because of mine, I went to Poppleton Park with Dale, Alex, Charlie and Don to fly our red and black dragon kite. Do you remember what the storeowner told me about that kite? He said that it was designed to frighten away evil spirits and attract good ones. I thought about that on the way to the park.

But the wind was light and variable, and I couldn't get the kite to stay up in the air, until I remembered how you used to do it. You used to run with the kite until you got it above the tree line, where the wind could take it the rest of the way. How I loved to watch you run! You seemed to just relish the pure freedom of it, your arms and legs straining themselves to their limits, the wind in your face and hair, and your feet almost airborne.

So I ran and I thought of you. And the kite went up. Then I saw two birds fly out of a tree to the west of the field and circle around the kite, now bobbing and fluttering in the light breeze. Diving and swooping, the birds frolicked with that kite. Then, the wind stopped and the kite fell to the ground in a graceful swoon, and the birds followed it down. They continued to dive at it playfully and circle above it while it was lying on the ground, and they stayed nearby while I got the kite up in the air again. The birds played with the kite the whole time I flew it. I have never seen anything like it before or since.

It felt like a message from you. It felt as though your spirit did not die, and it had been here with me. I felt warm inside. I felt a temporary relief from the harshness of my pain. I knew that it was the beginning of a long road.

Love,
Dad

July 14, 1990

Dear Andrew,

I have to tell you … your room, the room we designed together for you, has to be changed. Eventually, it will become the baby's room, but that is too large a transition for me. Linda suggested that we just empty it first. So, before it becomes the baby's room, it will be no one's room. And we will have a ceremony in the emptied bedroom to remember you, and your place.

But, I must clean it out before that is possible, before it can be nobody's room. And how can I do that? It feels like one more proof that you are never coming back. You won't need your bed or your toys, because you're gone. I tell you, I have the same empty feeling that I had immediately after you died. I feel a hollow place that starts somewhere in my chest and extends all the way to my soul, and, inside, all along the cavity, the edges are raw and on fire. I feel the pain as an enormous weight in my bones that seems to render me immobile. I feel it as a choking heat in my throat that cuts off my words and makes me mute. For yet a part of me dwells in a future that will never bloom. I am cut off from the place in my heart that is already there, beckoning expectantly for me to catch up. Oh, it could have been so beautiful, and now it will never be, as I fear my very actions today confirm.

In the midst of all these thoughts and feelings, I look up from my imponderable task and I see you sitting on the bed, half turned away from me, your back and head bowed. You are silent, as if sharing the dreadful import of this moment. How I long to talk to you! What do I say, that you will never grow up, never get bigger, never fall in love? I could go on and on with the list of "nevers", but then what more needs be said? It would seem almost as if I am justifying my actions in your room. Yes, I know that I've told you this before, but I guess I now understand it myself at a deeper level. It is the same as before, but not the same, so maybe I need to say it again.

But, you give no response. After all, what response is there to give? What is there for you to say to this, the worst news imaginable? And yet, I am angry for a moment. Talk to me! Tell me what happened when you died. I want answers. I want to know! I need to know. And then my storm passes.

Oh, Andrew, I'm sorry that I react so. I don't want anger to come between us, but I have so much anger inside me that it just seems to erupt sometimes. And I am struggling with so many things. For a while, I have been grappling with the events of your death. Sometimes I think that I don't care if I know what happened. Sometimes I think I know, and sometimes I know that I don't, but I want so badly to know. It all just goes around and around.

No, let us just sit together, you and I, the way we used to. We needn't say anything at all. And then, time stands still, at least for this moment.

But, I must climb out of the calm depths of our shared solitude and return to the reason I am in your room. Andrew, the truth is, I can't face parting with your toys, your furniture, your stuff! It feels as though I'm "getting rid" of things, of reminders. Without them, I'm afraid that I'll forget you. I'm afraid that I'll forget how you looked, how you sounded, how you smelled. I'm afraid that I'll forget to remember you.

I can't face that this is goodbye, and that I'll never see you again. I can't face that we'll never hug again. I keep seeing your tear-stained cheeks.

And now, now that I must face what I cannot, what am I going to do with your unfinished models, or your models barely begun, much like your life? What am I going to do with your toys, in which years of play yet remain?

What am I going to do with your socks? What am I going to do with your one shoe? What am I going to do?

    Love,
    Dad

July 29, 1990

Dear Andrew,

I have been having such a hard time writing this letter. Linda and I have finished taking apart your room. We put away memorabilia, collected a few toys and we gave away the rest. We even disassembled your bed. In the end, I felt better knowing that your things would not go to waste. Some other child would enjoy them. Who would ever have guessed that that child would not be you? I could not have done it without Linda. Alone, I was completely overwhelmed by even the smallest decisions. With her, I could see what was important for me to keep and what I could let go.

At night, I dreamed a dream without pictures. It was just the sound of my voice saying over and over, "Andrew's never coming back. Andrew's never coming back." In this time, I have re-experienced all of the feelings I have had since you died. I have felt intense rage, helplessness, emptiness, purposelessness, and, finally, a sense of loss that is so deep that it seems beyond words and even beyond tears. I have not wanted to do this, and then to know what I now know more deeply than ever, that you're never coming back. I was prepared even to pick up and move to a new house to avoid taking apart your room. I guess it has also been the dismantling of your dream, the secret laboratory.

The room is empty now. We have given away your bed, your desk and chair and your chest. You see, to me, they would always be yours. Who else could use them? Who else could own them? No one who lives with me. There is an echo now in the empty room you used to fill. If I left your things, that echo would ring in my heart through the furniture and toys that used to be yours. None of us, Linda, the baby or I, could live with that.

And I have learned a lot in the last weeks. I have learned how much personal choice affects our lives. In the past, I have known that we often decide whether or not we will survive, and beyond that whether or not we will truly live. I remember making the choice to live at Camp Walden, three months after your death. But, until now, I hadn't realized the extent to which our lives are shaped by all of our decisions. Now, I have learned that we decide whether or not we will learn and grow from new experiences. I have learned that we decide whether or not we will feel. And now I have learned that we must make these decisions every day, over and over. Once is not enough. For during these weeks, I have had to decide again and again to live, to feel, to grow.

I have been stuck in my grief for you. I now see my mourning process as a struggle between my wanting you to come back, and my knowing, nay my feeling, that you won't. I could not move toward accepting that you're never coming back. It was too painful. I didn't want to. Your room was both a reminder of your absence and a hope for your return. How many times I could walk by your room and not even see it! That's how badly I wanted to not face your loss.

And yet, I have been aware for some time that things have changed. I have not wanted to be aware, but I have been. For so long, it was a comfort to me that you would appear to me, that I could feel your hugs and see your smile. But it has been about a year that I have felt a difference in you. You have moved on to something new. Your visits, like the one a few weeks ago, have become extremely rare. And I need to let you go, both for you and for me. I feel it is time.

It has been quite a while that, when I let my thoughts just wander to you, I find myself transported to a remote locale, far from other people. I am walking in a forest, sheltered from the sun by a canopy of lush greenery. There is an eagle soaring aloft, so high it's almost out of sight. It is intermittently visible, occasionally obscured by the branches above. It is you. I just know it! And I see you circling about a nest, an inaccessible aerie, on a sheer cliff overlooking my forest. It is your home. You have made your own way. And, I am earthbound, far below and looking up, squinting into the sunlight and straining to catch a glimpse of you in your elegant flight. But, every so often, you swoop down toward me in a powerful dive, and our eyes meet then in silent communion, just for a moment, before you are gone again. You are so graceful and free, and I am so proud of you.

Go well, my son. Stay well.

Love,

Dad

August 15, 1990

Dear Andrew,

There has been a lawsuit -- Mom has sued the driver and her next-door neighbors. I'm not sure what the legal allegations were, perhaps negligence or wrongful death, or both. It doesn't matter. Win or lose, there is a cost to waging war, even if it's a "peaceful" war in a court of law. I don't know what price Mom has had to pay. I can only tell you about mine.

I don't mean to imply that the lawsuit was a bad idea. Quite the contrary. I was sympathetic with Mom's going ahead with the suit, but I didn't anticipate how painful it would be for me.

It began when Mom's lawyer asked if I would like to have a financial stake in the outcome. That is, he wanted me to add my claim to the action. In fact, he pressured me to try to get some money, because he said that it would strengthen the primary suit. I refused. It was tempting, because I am so angry, but I could not imagine what I would do with money that resulted from your death. I want to be clear. I never had a single doubt in my mind about taking money. I could not do it. That is my personal reaction, and I don't judge anyone else for choosing otherwise, but I could not. However, the mere fact that it was offered, that it was a possibility, was agonizing to me. I know that many people sue for revenge, but it certainly is not presented that way in court. I'm not sure that revenge as a motivation is healthy, in the long run, but I understand and sympathize with it as a human response to pain. Presumably, the larger the award granted by the court, the greater the sense of vindication by the plaintiff.

In the minds of the litigants, money then translates directly into an assessment of guilt.

But it doesn't work like that. Damages are always awarded on the basis of loss, and on the basis of what is called "pain and suffering". Therefore, a large part of the lawyers' job is to establish guidelines for those two factors, over and above proving culpability. For myself, I could not live with a process that places a dollar value on either one and I could not profit in so direct a manner from your death. I could not do it. I do not regret it.

Later, I was required to talk to the lawyer about what I saw, as preparation for my deposition. Deposition is a form of out-of-court testimony before the lawyers for all sides. It is recorded and under oath. I was not ready for what I was to feel the day of the deposition. Some people might have guessed that the testimony would recall such unpleasantness for me that I would sink back into grief and anger, but it didn't happen that way. I see the accident over and over every day, and my anger and grief are always present. No, that wasn't the issue.

You see, in talking with the lawyer, it became crystal clear to me for the first time that no one was interested in learning the truth of what happened that day, the day you were killed. Each lawyer sought only to represent the facts in a light favorable to his own client's best interests. I was but an actor in the lawyers' drama, not an informed witness who could clear up ambiguity. The truth was not a goal, but merely an instrument to create bias. Ambiguity served both sides. It was a kind of game, with its own rules of conduct for all participants. And because of that, what about the parts played by those not named in the lawsuit? None of that would be addressed. The guilty could continue to hide behind facades of respectability.

My rage at what happened to you two years ago was compounded by what was continuing to happen. Earlier that day, the day of the deposition, still at work, I could not hold it in and I had to go outside to my car where it was safe to scream at the top of my lungs. Perhaps screaming is a form of anger song. If so, I performed many choruses before my turn with the lawyers.

I don't know if my testimony was helpful to Mom's case. For her sake, I hope so. In fact, as often happens, the suit was settled out of court, so Mom did get a monetary award. Of course, the other aspect of a settlement is that usually, no one admits any responsibility, and that, too, happened. So, the lawsuit did not really establish anything about guilt. I wish it had.

My final act in this drama came because the check for the award was made out both to Mom and to me, and, of course, it belonged wholly to Mom. Accordingly, her lawyer brought the check and met me at my bank so that I could countersign it over to her. I don't remember why we needed the bank's services or why we had to wait, but we did, and I remember that, in making idle conversation, I said, "Of course, no amount of money could ever be enough." It seemed to me perfectly obvious that I was talking about the futility of putting a dollar value on a person's life. It seemed to me perfectly obvious that the natural response should have been, "Of course it couldn't." I don't know, perhaps he didn't understand what I was talking about. Perhaps he was stuck in some legal-technical loop. Perhaps. But, at his response, I had to wonder what kind of person does this for a living. What he told me, in summary, was the manner in which courts decide how much a particular human life is worth, in terms of earning potential and dependents, for example. I couldn't believe it. So, among other things, the monetary value of a deceased person is related to the monetary income of the once living person. And, of course, since you had no income and no dependents, your "value" was relatively low.

Even as I write this, I am sick to my stomach. The horror of your death seems to replicate itself in a curious caricature of a dance through our legal institutions and customs. I am so glad that I refrained from accepting any money from these people, from this process. The cost would have been far too high. It was high enough as it was.

Love,
Dad

September 28, 1990

Dear Andrew,

I have been in a sad, contemplative mood, Andrew. This has been a difficult time. Your new baby sister is due to be born any time now. I have been feeling her presence for a while. She is someone, an individual I have never met. And I feel myself bonding with her already. That feels warm, but also frightening for me. I have learned, over and over, how much I love, and how deeply I hurt when I lose someone I love. I am making myself so very vulnerable.

I have learned that never to love feels empty, much as to love and lose feels empty. But the former is the emptiness of a dry, unused glass, overlaid with the dust of discarded dreams. The latter is the emptiness of a drained mug of thick, sweet nectar, its sides still moist with poignant memories, at once the most fragile and the most durable of our possessions. Knowing does not make doing less frightening.

I am in the midst of an amazing and difficult passage. As I grieve your death, I am also poised to celebrate your sister's birth. Love, life, death. What else is there?

This fall, it seems to me that I have seen an unusual number of animals lying dead in the road, crushed by automobiles. I sense that most people simply ignore them. But I can't. Yes, they remind me of you. But I also wonder at what I am seeing -- all of these uselessly lost lives. Perhaps there is even more to this story, though. Often I see pairs of animals, killed side by side. Why would that happen?

A few weeks ago, I was driving on the freeway when I saw a bird lying dead in the middle of my lane. It is rare to see a bird hit by a car. It reminds me of the bird I hit just days before you were killed. But, much more astonishing to me, there was another bird of the same kind standing next to the dead one, seemingly unwilling to leave the side of its companion. I swerved a little and missed them both. I don't know if other drivers could do the same. I hope so. It seemed evident to me that the surviving bird was numb with grief and disbelief.

How can there be grief without love? Is this why death seems to visit the streets in pairs this fall? I think so. I love you.

Love,
Dad

October 26, 1990

Dear Andrew,

It's been a while since I've written, and yet, I've thought of you daily. On October 12, 1990, Hannah was born. You have a new baby sister, and, of course, that makes you a big brother. But, then, you already knew that, didn't you? Yesterday, I was holding Hannah on the sofa, in the den. She was sleeping on my chest and, as I closed my eyes, my thoughts drifted to you. How I used to hold you, heartbeat to heartbeat, as we sat in that same place! I can feel it yet.

And I thought of you, my little boy, and now, holding my new little girl, I felt so full and yet so empty at the same time. But then, suddenly, I became aware that you were there with us. You had been standing nearby, in the doorway, watching us. You were leaning over at the waist, as you so often did, and you were craning your neck to see Hannah. Your eyes were wide, an expression of curiosity and radiant wonder lighting your entire face. You stood like that, on your tiptoes, for quite a while, and then you walked softly over to us and bent over my knee to look more closely. Then, you reached out and gently stroked Hannah's head, and, in that instant, you were gone.

Hannah slept through your whole visit, curled lightly on my chest, rhythmically inhaling her breaths of life, as you used to do. You were once so vibrantly alive, as Hannah is today. Even now, after two and a half years, I don't understand how it can be that you live no longer. But, that is so.

And here is Hannah, as you have seen, little and helpless, and so dear to my heart, as you have been. And yet, she has a powerful life force in her that fairly screams aloud to me, "I am! I will be!" Such a large spirit in so small a body!

Andrew, what I feared most has not come about, nor do I now believe it will. I was afraid that, in my love for Hannah, I would forget you; that I would lose both my pain and my joy in you. Well, the opposite has happened. My love for you and for Leah has deepened. Indeed, my whole ability to love seems more profound. How is it possible?

Sometimes, I feel rendered to my inmost being with the intensity of feeling. How can I describe it, this pain, and this joy, this expanding of my very soul? Yes that is what it is, an expansion, and the scars I feel from past loss stretch only with complaint. Sometimes, I feel ground to dust and rebuilt anew. Oh, my old wounds are still there -- they remind me who I am and from whence I came -- but there is a new light to heal familiar shadows. And, as I grow new love for Hannah, I feel my heart enlarge for everyone I love.

I miss you more than ever.

Love,

Dad

January 29, 1991

Dear Andrew,

A week ago Saturday, Linda's Uncle George died of a heart attack, suddenly and unexpectedly. We have had many deaths since you were killed. This was the first one that, like yours, was a shock. Oh, death seems always to be a surprise, even when it has been long awaited, but sometimes, as with you and with Uncle George, well, your deaths somehow seem to violate some natural order. Uncle George was 61, and people spoke of how young he was. But, my God! How young you were!

At the funeral, I was back with you, with your horrible death, your ghastly funeral. And, as the priest spoke about Uncle George, I realized that I need to say goodbye to you. The thought of "goodbye" brings my tears from some deep well inside me. I have noticed different qualities to my tears. Mere sadness causes tears like drops over the brim -- a simple spill. But, overwhelming sorrow, loss that bleeds my soul, causes tears that seem to emanate from my entire body. Even thinking about saying "goodbye" to you seems to transform my whole self into such tears. Deep down, I feel that I never before believed I could survive "goodbye".

Oh, I know, I have done little "goodbyes", sometimes in my dreams, and then bigger ones with the help of friends. I have even cleaned up and rededicated your room, a major "goodbye". But, I have, until now, avoided saying anything like a final "goodbye" to you. Maybe I thought I had said "goodbye" already -- certainly my reaction to the funeral came as a surprise to me. But, I do know that I'm still angry, and your death still hurts.

What will it mean to me, to you, to us? I don't know. I'm having a hard time imagining. I can't imagine ever forgetting you. I can't imagine ever loving you less than I do right now. So, what will it mean?

Last night, Lila graduated from group, and said "goodbye". It feels right, the natural thing, and I'm happy for her. Yet, I'm sad for the ending to a long and rewarding association with Lila in group. I am leaving group soon -- lots of endings for me.

Your death was not right or natural, and it will always feel that way to me. How much harder to mark our ending! So, what will it mean? Perhaps, there is no "final" ending. Perhaps each "little" ending is but a step in the grief process -- a part of gradually accepting the unacceptable. Perhaps, but it feels like each little ending is so final, and I'm not ready.

Love,
Dad

May 2, 1991

Dear Andrew,

I have left grief group. It is almost the eve of the third anniversary of your death, and I am risking another ending. It is an odd feeling, to be done with grief group but not with grief. Yet, it is so. On the one hand, I will miss the group, and on the other, I am taking it with me, in spirit and in healing, but also in friendship.

I have become close friends with Jan, who I met when I first went to grief group. In fact, that night, I think we both knew that we would become friends. Her daughter, Amy, died about one month before you did, and we found ourselves feeling many similar emotions during the whole next year or so in the group, but we had many other connections than that -- shared interests in music, shared values, shared views. It is an irony that first death changed my life through loss and then the people I met to deal with that loss further changed my life. Even knowing what had to happen to bring Jan into my life, I can no longer imagine my life without her friendship.

Aside from Jan, what did I get from the group? It's hard to say what were the most important aspects -- there were so many. What comes to mind at once is the sense of shared pain from the members as a whole, an awareness that drives out the bitter certainty of isolation in a world suddenly gone desolate. For this alone, the group was worthwhile, but there was more. Certainly, there was support for the unique areas of my process, as well as validation for the aspects of my grief process that were common to others. Hearing the similarities of experience, even when circumstances varied widely, helped me to know that what I was feeling was not only not crazy, but actually expected given what has happened in my life.

Sometimes, we discussed ways for dealing with difficult times, such as anniversaries, or awkward situations. You would be surprised at how painful a formerly benign social interaction can be. For example, what do I say when someone asks me, "How many children do you have?" If I say "two", meaning just Leah and Hannah, then I feel that I have abandoned you, and I feel that I have been unfaithful to the truth inside me. After all, aren't you one of my three children?

On the other hand, if I say "three", how do I handle the inevitable, "Oh, how old are they?" In this case, there seems to be no way to avoid telling a relative stranger the most intimate and sensitive part of my life, "My son died in 1988." Never mind the fact that I have now made myself vulnerable, I have also put this other person, who merely asked a seemingly innocent question, in the position of having to acknowledge and deal with death. Does that make me responsible for someone else's potential discomfort? Over time, the group helped me to see that I was not responsible, and I learned to be comfortable with a response that addressed both my internal and external realities: "I have three children, two living and one deceased."

When I started going to group, it was shortly after your death, and the group gave me a lot of support. I felt that I myself was able to give very little. Slowly though, over time, I was able to give back to the group, both to old and new members -- to share their sorrow and to aid in any way I could, even just to listen. Uncritical listening is sometimes the greatest gift we can give ... and receive. Perhaps giving is a prerequisite to healing.

It is sad for me to leave the group, after all we have meant to each other. So, why leave now? This is not an easy question to answer. I think that when each of us first came to grief group, we were lost and hurting. Our assumptions, our future, our world, all had been torn away in an agonizing moment, whether through illness or violence, and we each needed to find a new path and new meanings. Here in group, what we found was a community of lost souls, each searching in our own way, and somehow, we found nurture and courage in the fellowship.

Did the group give us what we really wanted when we came? Did it provide the answers we sought? Did it tell us what path to take? No, it didn't. But, if the group was not what I wanted, because in fact that was not possible, at least it was what I ultimately needed. If it didn't provide the answers I craved, at least it did provide a place where I could ask my questions freely. And if it didn't light a path for me to follow, at least it did guide me in my individual quest. I believe that it did the same for most of the others in the group, as well. Far from offering false hope and empty promise, rather it spoke lovingly to my heart and my soul, so that they could begin to heal. At the time, it nourished me in a way no other human contact could.

You know, when the spirit has been emptied, it yearns for filling, and like an empty stomach that counts the minutes to the next meal, my soul counted the days until the next nurturing group meeting. So it was in the beginning, and for several years. What I have now come to realize is that my heart no longer marks the time between meetings. Perhaps my spirit has been nurtured enough by the group, and now requires a different sort of sustenance. Perhaps, having found a path with the help of the community, my spirit needs to travel that path alone. Sometimes, a flower seed requires a special soil in order to germinate, but then must be transplanted before it can achieve full maturity. Perhaps, like that seed, I must leave my special garden to enable my process to continue. Yet, how strange it is to say "good-bye" to the very association that has helped me so crucially with "good-byes"! And how sad it is to leave this place of sorrow!

It is time. I sense it is time. I wonder who, besides myself, I will meet around the next bend in this road.

I miss you.

Love,

Dad

September 15, 1991

Dear Andrew,

In a few days, it will be your 12th birthday. How far removed we are from your last birthday, when we celebrated together! How big would you be? What would your interests be? What would you be like? Impossible! I find myself imagining all sorts of different possibilities and they are all impossible. Impossible possibilities ... You're still 8 years and 8 months old. You're still the same size. You're still the same.

Yet I am changed. Oh, yes, I am older, and also sadder, but I am a fuller person, too -- I am more full of feeling than ever before. I have more joy and more sorrow, more anger and more calm -- I should say not just more, but deeper. And I live a strange paradox. At the same time, I feel more connected to people than ever before, but also I am more aware of my separateness.

Sure, I am separate in the same way we all are, alone in our bodies, secluded in our thoughts and reactions. But, sometimes I feel like an alien in my own culture. Let me explain. Ours is not a culture that is particularly tolerant of grief. We don't like mourning endings, only celebrating new beginnings. Even leaving a good job for a better one involves commemorating both an ending and a beginning, yet we eschew the former. Our fear of endings, of death, shows up in our language.

We don't often speak plainly of death and dying. Instead, we soften it and say that someone has "passed away" or "passed on". Where? Sometimes, we say that we have "lost" someone. I have said it myself, but I always feel strange afterwards. Some people say that their beloved dead are "sleeping", which, I have heard, can frighten children when it's time for bed. Then, there are what I call the traveling euphemisms -- our loved one has "left" us, or is "gone" or "departed". Finally, there are more religious substitutes, like "gone to heaven", "in eternal rest", or "gone to their final reward". Oh, wait, there is my personal favorite: "gone to a better place". I guess if I knew you had gone to a better place, there would be no need for me to mourn, only to celebrate.

I once met a mother in grief group whose son had died, but who could not say the so-called "d" word, even years after her loss, and I perceived her to be in a perpetual state of struggle and suffering, which she manifested by exhibiting a bizarre and uncomfortable humor. Yet, how could she grieve when it was too painful for her even to admit the need? How could she live when the painful reality of her loss stood between her and everything else? For years, she had been stuck in limbo between two insurmountable walls of agony. Words are important, both as symbols and as tools.

However, my story about euphemisms is only half over, for our recognition and fear of the finality of death spills over into less threatening areas. And spill it does. Many of the words and phrases I have collected have their origins in circumstances befitting their seriousness, but they have been accepted lightly into everyday language.

A "deadline" used to be a line in the Confederate prison Andersonville, during the Civil War, that prisoners crossed at peril to their lives. Now, we use the term to mean a due date. Another such phrase is "drop dead date". When we're very tired, we say that we're "dead tired" or "just dead". When we sleep deeply, we say that we're "dead to the world". We can be either "dead wrong" or "dead right". A tie is called a "dead heat" and an impasse is called a "deadlock". A street with no outlet is called a "dead-end" and, presumably, if you were following directions, you could find what you're looking for by going "dead ahead".

A radio or television station that is not broadcasting is sending "dead air" and, I would guess, if you tuned in you would hear "dead silence". If the wind is not blowing, you would experience "dead calm", and that might most likely occur in the "dead of night". Having no expression on your face, especially in a comic attempt (!), is called a "dead pan" and, if you were found in the act of doing something wrong, you would be caught "dead to rights". It is a mystery to me that when you capture something perfectly, an idea for example, it is said that you got it "dead nuts".

Most of the casual phrases I've written only bother me to the extent that people seem to use them unconsciously, but the next few actually upset me. I don't know what else to say about them. There is nothing left but to write them: "if I do such and such, so and so will kill me!", meaning, "so and so will be unhappy with me"; "I could kill for a … ", meaning, "I really want … "; "that's just murder", meaning, "that's terrible". I hate it most of all, though, when people talk about "road kill", or, intending that they don't feel well, when they say, "I feel as though I was hit by a Mack truck!"

With our language the way it is, I suppose it's no surprise that most people expect that grief, however deep and painful, will be essentially over within a few weeks, and that then the mourner will "move on". After all, there are new beginnings to conquer, new doors to open. Certainly, but I wonder if each of us can only tolerate so much unresolved, unexpressed grief before we get stuck. Perhaps, we store a well inside that becomes further laden with sorrow with every unmourned loss.

At a certain point, that well becomes full. There is no more room for sadness and, therefore, we cannot voluntarily take on another ending without first draining the well, which we often fear to do. And if this is the case, how can we turn toward another beginning, when to begin something new requires the ending of something old? There is no space for it.

Certainly there are new doors to open, and I have opened some myself. I'm sure that I will open more. But grief has changed me. It has made my well deeper, my ken stronger and my anger more focused. It has at once tried my spirit and strengthened it. I know that I have further to go in my own grief, although I'm not sure what the next steps will be. I also know that euphemisms and platitudes do not comfort me. Quite the contrary. They reinforce my separateness, ironically at the very time I need closeness.

Happy birthday, my son! I miss you.

Love,

Dad

March 1, 1993

Dear Andrew,

I have left General Motors. I was there, at the Research Labs, for a long time -- just about 16 years. I worked for GM all your life. Actually, I resigned about six months ago to start my own company, RD International, or RDI, for short.

Leaving GM was not easy for me. You couldn't know it, but I had been thinking of leaving for several years, so it took me some time before I could actually leave. Perhaps if I had gone to a different traditional job, working for an established company, it would not have been so hard, but the truth is, I didn't really know what I wanted in my career. I didn't have a direction.

Then, in the summer of 1992, Dale and I began talking about starting our own company -- there were several things we could have designed our company to do, but it's not important to tell you about them now. What is important is that I found the idea of partnering with a dear friend to be irresistible, and, in August, I left GM.

Certainly, I was excited about my new prospects, running my own company with Dale, but I was also sad. General Motors had been good to me and good for me during our years together. The Research Labs supported my ideas with money and with personnel, and, in turn, my inventions were validated by the teams I led. Over the years, my self-confidence grew. In addition, the people who were my closest colleagues were friendly and caring, and supremely patient in the months and years after your death. I will miss them.

So, I hear you ask, why did I leave? Good question. Well, I grew tired of the limitations corporate policies placed on what I could do, what I could investigate. I grew tired of the seemingly endless meetings that never seemed to converge. Most of all, though, I grew tired of living with the value conflict I felt in working for a car company. I have never liked cars, but the problem goes deeper than that. I have always been disturbed by the fact that, while cars grant freedom and flexibility for their owners, they do so at an enormous cost to the environment and to our natural resources. Now, however, I have a deeper issue with cars. While I know that cars have been of great value in society, as emergency vehicles, for example, I also know that they kill people -- one killed you -- and they kill other innocent creatures. I have not known how to resolve this, and I still don't. I remain uneasy about it, though.

Well, I guess that's a short description of the road that led me off the staff of GM and into a leadership position in my own company, but what does my company do? Well, initial explorations of some of the possibilities came up empty -- all, except one. About one month after I left GM, some of my friends there approached me about continuing my robotics work in the context of a particular factory application. Sure, I had conflicts about working with GM again, even though I would no longer be an employee, and I had concerns about sustaining a line of research and development that had become tiresome for me. On the other hand, this would be a practical implementation, not a lab demo, and it promised to be the challenge of a lifetime for me. Something inside of me cried out for fulfillment -- the completion of a dream of more than a decade, the commercialization of the ideas I first discovered at the time of your birth. I could finally build a product, a robot control system, with all of the capability I had foreseen for years. It would be my great adventure.

Do I still have a value conflict? Yes, and it still brings disquiet, but, somehow, I have not been able to resist this opportunity. Perhaps there is too much of me and my past in it. Perhaps there is too much of you and our past in it. Perhaps, one day, I'll know.

What I do know, however, is that I am engrossed in my work more than ever before in my career. My creativity is in high gear, my passion is fully engaged, and the days just seem to fly by. No longer do I toil to prove in a laboratory what I already know instinctively -- that my inventions work on yet another robot with yet another kind of motor. Now my work does not feel like work, but, then again, it does not feel like play either. Somehow, in building this new control system, I am exploring my own depth and breadth of expression, and so the question is not so much what I am doing, but how I am being.

Oh, and when I have questions, or need advice, I am working with good friends at GM who have been fully supportive. Indeed, the plan is to test the prototype and to tune it first in a laboratory with equipment on loan from the manufacturing plant, and then to install the final version on the production equipment in the plant. I feel unaccustomed optimism about this project.

By the way, one of the advantages of my new career is that I am working primarily at home, and so that means that I get to share a great many "accidental" moments with Hannah. I wish I had had more of those times with Leah, and with you.

I miss you.

Love,

Dad

May 19, 1993

Dear Andrew,

Today, it is five years since you were killed, and I am struggling with so many feelings. At times, my rage at the circumstances of your life and death seems bottomless, and my pain at your loss is its constant companion. At other times, I feel numb with disbelief at the passage of time. Once, in the early days and months after your death, time seemed to creep with glacial deliberation, as I stared into space and saw nothing but loss and emptiness. Then, the chasm of time widened into a canyon of aching and longing. And now those structured moments have added up to five whole years. It seems as unbelievable to me as the fact that the oceans are made up of individual drops of water.

And my anger has not softened. Sometimes, I feel as though I know what other people were thinking and doing that day, that terrible day, and that I know the story behind the story of what happened to you. How do I know? I tell you, I just know. And then, of course, I want everyone to know what I "know"!

Here is what happened. Your next-door neighbor, Nate, was jealous of your relationship with me for reasons that are worth examining. Why were you playing with Nate? Well, commonly, if you were already playing with Nate when I arrived to pick you up, you either delayed or, sometimes, you refused to come with me at all. It had long been an issue that had even spilled over into court. When you waved to me as I drove up, Nate became extremely angry, and, moments later, he purposefully pushed you into the street on his wagon. The driver of the truck that killed you saw you enter the street and became angry that "some kid is playing in the street". He decided that he would give you a scare by passing extremely close to you. You clung to the sides of the wagon, frozen with fear to find yourself in the street. Seconds later, the various miscalculations converged and you were dead.

Here is what happened. Your next-door neighbor, Nate, grew up alone in the street with very little concept of his own "street sense", or perhaps your relative lack of it. Why were you playing with Nate? Could any difficulty between us at visitation pick-up time be reported in court? I'm not sure, but, perhaps, to avoid contact with me that she considered unpleasant, Mom sent you to play with Nate while she talked on the telephone in the back of the house, out of sight. Because of his experiences, Nate had no idea what might happen when he pushed you so hard into the street. The driver, upset over the imminent loss of his failing business and his failing marriage, was driving largely unconsciously down the street. Your presence in the street did not register on him at all. Within moments, all of our lives unraveled, as the earth seemed to open up and swallow you.

Here is what happened. Months and months of emotional trauma were making you crazy. However, several weeks before your death, the adults in your life, your teacher and others, reported that you suddenly seemed at peace. Had you made a decision? It is said that a child in unimaginably painful circumstances must either repress feelings, or die. You were constantly faced with choosing between two parents, two warring parties, both of whom you loved. It was an impossible choice, and you expressed your feelings of desperation and anger frequently to me. That expended one option. And so, when I dropped you off on Tuesday and said, "See you Thursday," you replied, "Wanna bet?", your last words to me. And your wave when I first saw you that last Thursday was really to say "goodbye". There was no need for you to steer the wagon. It was to be your final ride. There was no need for you to look down the street. You knew what was coming. We both did. I had even warned you about it ahead of time. So many people had failed to see you, the divorce judge, lawyers, the guardian ad litem, educators, yes, and even me, how surprising could it be that you were killed by a driver who probably didn't see you? Oddly, in spite of the pain, I'm grateful that we shared your last moments.

Here is what happened. At one time or another, a lot of us failed you, some of us more than others, but all of us nevertheless. Listen, Andrew. In retrospect, I have realized that one of the reasons I went to bereavement support groups was to listen to parents' stories and to try to find a pattern. "Why did these parents lose children?" I sought to discover. "Why did I lose a child?" Was it because of some overwhelming abuse or some series of parenting mistakes that somehow triggered the tragic deaths of these children? What I learned is that the parents who lost children were no worse (and no better) at parenting than others whose children have not yet died. I found no pattern, no reason. Rather, each life and each death was unique.

Here is what happened. All of what I have described is what happened ... and more things besides.

Look, Andrew, here is what happened ... I guess I don't really know what happened. I know a lot of facts. I know what I saw, heard and felt. I know, right or wrong, what my intuition tells me. And I know that I miss you more than anything, and that your memory brings me warmth, and an aching sadness. But what, then, is the truth?

Perhaps what I have been searching for doesn't exist. Perhaps, in the fabric of our lives, there is no truth that stands like a monument, proof against time. Perhaps there are only truths, like patches, that we weave together as well as we can into rough-fitting garments that we wear in layers. The outer ones get the most notice and the most wear, while the inner ones determine our ultimate comfort.

But they serve, at least until we have utterly and undeniably outgrown them. Then, discarding the frayed and threadbare parts, we reweave, and we layer afresh; new patches, new weaving, new layers, new meanings.

But I love you constantly. Go well, my son. Stay well.

Love,

Dad

August 6, 1993

Dear Andrew,

Perhaps all my life, I have searched for meaning. This predisposition, this need, seems to come from some deep reservoir within me. How can I describe it? I don't know. All I know is that, since you were killed, that need has grown to the level of an obsession. I seem often to be thrown back into fundamental questioning. I ask myself, again and again, what is life all about? What meaning can there be to all of this activity we pursue from birth to death? And why do so many others seem untroubled by these questions, which are so critical to me? I have come up against a brick wall, much like the wall of my dream after you were killed.

I think that there is no meaning, no purpose, independent and self-supporting. All is what we make of it. Your life and your death have meaning if I make it so. Perhaps I can bear witness to what I have seen, and to what I know. Perhaps I can pass along and share some of my passion for life lived fully, which grew under your influence. Perhaps I can give to others through example, the love and respect I feel for children. Perhaps I can give love to other little boys.

Perhaps I can teach that, if you lose someone or something that you love, then your life is changed forever. There is no going back, no returning to "normal".

Perhaps I can teach that, if you choose to engage in war, however personal and private, however seemingly "nonviolent", whatever you fight over will be destroyed. Perhaps I can teach that what life we have, what life surrounds us, what diversity confronts us, are all part of an unimaginably precious elixir. And that we dare not squander a drop of it if we are to be whole ourselves, for we are all connected through our living, indeed, through every breath.

Lately, Andrew, in the quiet, still moments of my soul, perhaps in the early morning, when the world is not quite awake, I occasionally hear you call "Dad!" Your sweet, high voice echoes inside me, "Dad!" It is almost a question. It is as if we have become separated in a department store, you on one aisle, me on another, and you have looked around the corner to make sure I am still near. "Dad!" Are you just checking in?

I am here, Andrew. I will always be here.

Love,

Dad

May 11, 1994

Dear Andrew,

It has been a long time since I have written, but you have been with me constantly. This has been the sixth year since you were killed. It seems unimaginable to me that so much time has passed. Sometimes, I feel as though it was last week.

And I must talk to you about something. It has been inside me for a long time, growing, trying to get out, and the words were not ready. Maybe now, they are.

When you were very little, we used to talk about how you would be when you grew up. I told you that you would probably be bigger than me, and I believed it. You laughed. The idea seemed so ludicrous to you. How could you ever be bigger than me? And yet, you were pleased. How wonderful it would be to be larger!

And you would go to school, and grow to be a man, in so many ways. And you would move out, and have a family of your own, and maybe some children who would call you "Dad". The words were just part of everyday conversation, flowing naturally and without thought. This would be the normal course of events. You knew it. I knew it. After all, growing up was your right, as a child, as a person.

But, we were wrong. I was wrong. I told you things that would not happen. I promised what I could not deliver. I didn't do it on purpose, but that hardly matters. It's my job, as your Dad, to tell you the truth, no matter how unpleasant, no matter how uncomfortable, and I have not been able to tell you until now. I have always seen you, your face dissolved in tears, and I could not face you with the truth. I have held that image inside me since the first days after you were killed. And, it is almost to that time that these thoughts are directed.

Andrew, you will not grow up. In your short lifetime, you will not experience manhood and independence. You will not experience romance or fatherhood. You will not experience spiritual awakening or emotional liberation. In this life, you will not have much of a chance. The words weigh as though they were lined with lead. They sink to the bottom of my soul where they dwell forever.

It is a father's job to protect his children. There are so many dangers, and, I see now that it is relatively easy to skirt the apparent ones. I can guard against death from the outside to some extent. But, sometimes I think that we each have a little death within us, held at bay by our fundamental life force. Perhaps, in spite of outward appearances, that is a fragile balance, at best.

Could it be that your life force weakened? Could it be that your life became so painful that your own internal call to death became undeniable? If so, neither I, nor anyone else could have saved you. If not on May 19, 1988, then you would have died some other day.

Sometimes, that's how it feels to me. I'm sorry that I contributed to the pain in your life. I'm sorry for some of the decisions I made that hurt you. I'm sorry for the ultimate price you paid.

As ever, love,
Dad

November 10, 1997

Dear Andrew,

This has been a difficult time for me in many ways, especially professionally. My company, RDI, has failed. After all the work I devoted, after all the time and money I invested, the company is dead. In spite of all the years of optimism surrounding my research and my accomplishments, General Motors has withdrawn support.

Once, we were partners, admittedly the collaboration of the minnow and the whale. Once, GM planned to fund my developments. It is not as though our technology failed; quite the contrary. We demonstrated successes well beyond anyone's expectations, but, apparently, it was not enough for GM. Instead, at the 25th hour, they wanted us to partner with another company, but, at the same time, they denied us permission to make videotapes of our accomplishments. Without hard evidence, forming a new alliance is, as a rule, next to impossible. And it didn't happen.

So, now RDI has had no income. I have lost money, both for myself and for our investor. And the opportunity to commercialize my invention, our invention, is gone. It had been my dream to make practical the ideas that first crossed my consciousness in 1979, the year you were born. What an integrated vision I had evolved for industrial automation, and, these last years, I finally realized that vision in software and hardware. It was the most challenging and absorbing professional project I ever attempted, and I did it. And now, is there nothing to do but to drop it? I am so disappointed and angry at the same time. I can't begin to tell you my depth of feeling. This work, this dream, this vision has been more than a job, more than a mere living. It has been my creation, a piece of myself.

I go to industrial shows and I see products on display, products that perform similarly to mine, but not as well, and I wonder, "Why couldn't this be my work on display? Why couldn't my inventions be shown here?" And now I don't know what to do.

My dream has failed. What do I do next? Sure, I am changed by what I did, and I learned a tremendous amount in the process. I suppose I could consult, but I have never done something like that. How do I begin? Can I just pick myself up, dust myself off and announce that I'm a consultant now? How do I bounce back from the end of a dream that spanned nearly two decades?

And now, all the time I am writing this, about GM, about automation, about RDI, I am aware that you were a part of this dream, too. It speaks to me from every line, from every paragraph. In my mind and heart, you were connected, almost from birth, to the innovations and developments that played out in recent months. I'm sure that my motivations for pushing this project, both from within GM and from beyond, have been complex. But, somewhere in the mix, you were always there. And so this turn of events has been doubly heavy for me.

Well, perhaps because of all this history, I took part in a special event last weekend. I found myself participating with a group of people who had all undergone deeply painful experiences within the last year. As suggested by the leaders, I prepared by writing an angry letter to GM and, armed with my poison pen, I launched myself confidently into the meeting. I had every right to be confident. After all, I knew that I would tell the story that I have related to you, although perhaps in greater detail. I knew that I would have a chance to express my outrage and my frustration. I knew that I would get a lot of support for my feelings. I just knew how it would go. I was certain.

Well, certainty can be a powerful force, but sometimes it charges forward blindly, and then is easily thrown by the weight of its own misdirection. That is what happened to me. It's not that the entire encounter with GM did not anger me. It did and it does. It's not that I was not disappointed. I was and I am. It's just that these feelings apparently paled compared to others that I had been too distracted, too preoccupied, too absorbed to notice. They had been growing inside me for several years and, until other people began to voice their own losses, I didn't know what I had been hiding from myself. But, then, with the opening words from the very first speaker, my emotions began to bubble up, buoyed by my own astonishment. My letter, my plans for the group, all went by the wayside in deference to my now undeniable feelings. I could hardly wait for my turn to speak, and then to let it all out.

You see, my hidden feelings were about you. Over the last several years, things have changed. It used to be that, on your birthday and on May 19, I had lots of phone calls and letters: "I'm thinking of you," or, "I'm remembering ... " Now, maybe, I get one or two. It seems to me that our anniversary has been all but forgotten. Maybe it's too much to expect that even my closest friends would remember after so many years. Maybe, but it hurts nonetheless.

It used to be that people would ask me about you -- about your early childhood, what you were like -- and they would recollect what they knew of you. It used to be that I felt you were included in my relationships, if only in memory. Now, I often feel that I am alone in remembering that you lived at all. Maybe it's too much to expect, after so many years. Maybe, but it contributes to my sense of isolation.

Perhaps worst of all, there is no one else who really experienced you, so that I could share memories of times past. Oh, yes, we used to get together with some of my friends, and, when prompted, they remember those occasions with pleasure, but it's not the same. What we shared together, you and I, especially in the last two years, we shared alone. Indeed, even if willing, Mom would not recall the same Andrew that I do because our perceptions of you diverged long ago, years before the divorce. So, I have come to feel that I alone keep your memory alive, in a world that continues to move on.

How difficult this has been for me to do! You see, there was a time, long ago, when I held you in my arms and you smiled up at me, your protector. Then, that time was past and it was replaced by another time, a time when you learned to walk and to talk. And then that time was past and it was replaced by another and yet another. Then came the end to those times ... Had you lived a normal life, I know that I would have to deal with that passing, but May 19 makes it all different. Your death so young puts a cloud of black over every one of those early memories. I can't help it. Even happy memories are colored by what I now know was the future you never had. How can I keep your memory alive when I am struggling with so much, and when the stain of the accident is often fresher to me than anything that came before? How can I keep you alive, when you have been dead for over eight years?

In the meantime, the earth continues to revolve indifferently, and sometimes, I feel so alone.

Love,
Dad

January 5, 1998

Dear Andrew,

It is another new year without you. It was ten years ago when we last celebrated New Year's Day together. Do you remember? For some reason, I now realize that you have been dead longer than you were alive. It's been true for a while, actually—since January 19, 1997. I'm not sure why that should have been such a shock to me, but it was.

Maybe it's all a trick of time. It simply can't have been so long since your death, can it? Or, is it that your life was so short? Or, is it both? How does the time pass for you? In a normal world, you would be going on 19 years old this year, and, right now, you would be entering your second semester in college. I can't believe it! In my mind, you are still eight years old. Sadly, it is not a normal world.

Maybe it is all a trick, but it's an undeniable trick. I have other evidence of the passage of time. Hannah will be eight years old this October. Yes, she is getting to be quite a young lady. Soon, she will be requesting, nay, demanding, greater freedom, more independence. She will be wanting to roam the neighborhood by herself. She will be ready to cross the street on her own. It is her right. She needs to continue to grow up.

It's my job to help her, and I will. I must. But, I tell you, the prospect fills me with terror because I know what can happen out there, in the blink of an eye. Yet, I do Hannah no favors if I hold her back. Someday, she must navigate this uncertain world on her own, and it is my responsibility to help her do it competently and confidently. And, in any case, who am I to think that I could protect her? Yet, I cannot deny my fear.

It doesn't help that, soon, she will be the same age you were when you were killed. I don't know why that should matter. Eight is not a curse, any more than any other age. Just because you were killed at eight doesn't mean that Hannah is especially vulnerable at eight. Yet there it is.

Hannah knows that I am afraid -- how could she not know? She also knows, in a general sense, what happened to you. I think that I have helped her to understand that she may be more ready for her independence than I am. I have tried.

I will continue to do what I can to teach her to manage her environment with respect, but without fear. The truth is that she is different from you in many ways. I know that. Still, it doesn't always help.

Go well, my son.

Love,

Dad

May 19, 1998

Dear Andrew,

Ten years! How do I comprehend this passage of time? How do I relate it to you? I have been feeling so much this month, and your death has been my almost constant companion. I wonder if I will ever find peace in my heart over your short life. I don't even know what that would mean. I do know that I will never be done shedding tears.

But this is the day, plus ten years. I'm not sure about today, but the weather may end up being similar to that one ten years ago. The weather was lovely, then, until late in the afternoon, when there were clouds and occasional light rain. Today, like that day, it has been lovely, and now, at almost 3:00 p.m., clouds are forming, and rain is predicted. This morning's paper reported that an 8-year-old girl was hit by a car and killed.

Linda and I went for a morning walk, our plan being to stop at the cemetery to visit your grave. There were freshly planted flowers. Who put them there? I always feel a sense of unreality in that cemetery, and yet, here I was, standing at your gravestone. Impossibly, it reads, "Andrew B. Goor, September 19, 1979 to May 19, 1988". I don't feel you here, in this quiet sanctuary from the busy road that serves it. I almost never do. Did you ever visit this place while you were alive? I doubt it.

If I associate you with a place, it is not this one. I realized, as I stood in the shade of this ancient plot, trying to make sense of what defies understanding, that my dominant memory of you is your death, and the span of time immediately preceding and following it. How can it be that, one moment you were safe on the sidewalk, waving an enthusiastic greeting to me as I arrived to pick you up, and the next moment, you were dead under the wheels of a black truck? Impossible. And yet, it is what happened. And happens again, as I remember.

And suddenly, as Linda and I walked slowly away from your stone marker with its incomprehensible message, a flood of memories washed over me. I remember how much joy you gave me, and also how frustrating you could be. I remember how gifted you were, and also how you were all boy -- physical, energetic and endlessly hungry. I remember your kindness and generosity, and I also remember your pain. I remember how much I learned from you when I thought that I was the teacher, and I remember that I never met anyone like you, before or since. In the meantime, the memories flow, like scenes from a beloved movie that ends too soon.

I remember how, even as a baby, you used to focus to such an extent on whatever you were doing that you never noticed your growing hunger. Then, suddenly, you would get so hungry that it seemed food could not be delivered fast enough through your tiny mouth to satisfy you. Now, the person feeding you was required literally to shovel the meal into you. And then, finally, the nourishment caught up with your need and you could slow down, and you began to kick your tiny feet rhythmically against the high chair. Until that moment, all of your energy and concentration were required to assure proper sustenance, but now, knowing that your body had what it needed, you could indulge in peripheral activity.

I remember that you always loved your big sister, Leah. I remember, when you were about three, that you met me at the door as I came home from work. You were so anxious to see me that you opened the door from the inside as I pushed it from the outside. You had a worried look on your face, and you said, "Leah's in trouble. Go kiss her!" Leah had been sent to her room, and you led me there so that I might help her.

I remember when you were about the same age, that you were riding in the car with Leah and one of her friends, who were being chauffeured to the movie theater to see "The Endless Story", and Leah was asked how long the movie was, so that we would know when to pick her up. Leah replied that the movie was about one and a half hours long. There was a long silence, which you broke with the question, "How can it be only an hour and a half if it's endless?" A very good question.

I remember how you used to frustrate Leah at Christmas because the two of you were so different. She loved to tear open her presents as fast as possible, to see what they all were. Later, she would look at each one appreciatively, but in the moment, she simply shredded the wrapping paper in a frenzy of discovery. You, on the other hand, faced by a veritable mountain of gifts, would just open one, and with no further thought to unwrapping, you would sit and play with that one present until you were satisfied and ready to open another. In an effort to egg you on, Leah would say, "Andrew, don't you want to open your other presents?" Apparently not yet.

I remember when you were a pre-toddler, crawling about the house. Did I say "crawling"? Perhaps I should have said, "careening". Sometimes you scooted so fast that you went around corners on two limbs, barely keeping your balance. And sometimes you would approach something that you knew you were not supposed to touch. You knew it. You would go up to it and reach for it, but then you would stop. You would turn around to see if I was watching, and if I was, you would smile, but without withdrawing your hand. If I said, "No, Andrew," you went closer, then stopped and smiled again. Eventually, I had to come pick you up to distract you from your original target. Or was the idea all along that I should pick you up? You could be such a rascal!

I remember how you loved to go up north to the cottage. You had freedom there and you could play with boats and you could dig in the sand. You didn't seem to care how cold the water was, or how rocky the beach. You went right in anyway, and squealed with delight.

I remember when you learned to walk, and now, suddenly, you could simply get up and go. And go you did! Sometimes, utilizing a moment's parental distraction, you would just disappear from the house. And where would you be found? In the backyard, climbing on the swing set. This was remarkable, because you were willing to climb higher than your much older sister would.

I remember that you always had your own unique view of the world, whether it was your fascination and understanding of concepts like "infinity", or your comprehension of the wafers in a Catholic chapel as "the body of God, you know, pretend", or your realization at three that, from now on, you would have to dress yourself because you were shown that "it said you could in the child book". I loved the words your infant tongue crafted, such as "grabity" to describe the force that keeps us all earthbound, that always seemed so appropriate. I was amazed that, at five, upon first getting an allowance, you quickly figured out how saving works, and you actually saved faithfully in your own little bank for almost a year to buy a toy jet plane.

I remember that, when you were seven, you wanted to learn to play chess, and I taught you. You caught on so quickly! You didn't just learn how to move the pieces. You seemed to grasp the essential strategy of the game, at a sophistication surpassing your years. Later, you went on to teach other children at Walden how to play chess. I know that they treasure that gift, as I treasure the memory of it.

I remember that you were always a very giving child. In fact, the first time I heard you say that you were going to lend a toy to a friend at school, I was going to advise you against it. Then, I thought, no, he will learn so much more when he never gets the toy back than I can teach him with words. But it was I who learned a lesson when, a month later, your friend returned your toy intact. In fact, you often lent toys to your classmates and invariably got them back. You explained it to me once, that a particular friend belonged to a family that could not afford many toys, and this friend did not have a basketball. So you lent him yours.

Once, when you were eight, and we were sledding, you and I were climbing the hill after a fast trip down. It was particularly cold and slippery, but you noticed a smaller girl on the hill behind us. She was dragging a sled that was too much for her, and the slope compounded her difficulties. She kept slipping and losing ground in her struggle up the hill. Even though you had your own sled in tow, you immediately went after her. You put her sled rope in one hand with your own and you held your free hand out to her for support. Together that way, the two of you made it to the top. I just watched you with pride and admiration.

I remember that, as you turned six or seven, you became more cautious than you were as a baby, and you always held my hand while crossing the street or while walking in parking lots. You would walk at my side, grasping my hand firmly until the last step or two, and then you would let go and jump, as if to say, "Safe!" How I wish I could hold your hand again, and say, "Safe!" How much more puzzling is your death! It's so hard for me to imagine that you were deliberately playing in the street that day.

I remember you at Walden summer camp. You became quite independent. You decided that you wanted to go to a peace workshop, even though I didn't want to go. You were swimming in the lake, but at the appropriate time, you got yourself out of the water, dried off and went to the workshop. After you were done, you returned with your peace project completed. I still remember the sight of you climbing the hill up to the cabins, walking in the noisy flip-flops that you wore for almost the entire week. It was not always easy for us there. You refused to eat most of the food that was served, and we sometimes had conflicting wants and needs. We were both struggling. But I remember how much you enjoyed arts and crafts, and playing chess.

I remember how snuggly you were -- you loved to climb into my lap for a long hug. You never outgrew your love for close contact. I remember how you wanted me to stay with you while you were falling to sleep. You liked me to lie next to you, either on the bed or on the floor, while holding your hand. I liked that, too.

I remember Sundays with you, after I had separated from Mom. We started off with waffles. I always asked what you wanted for breakfast and you always said the same thing – waffles. You must have liked them because there were never any left over. Then, what would we do for the rest of the day? It was always hard, because you wanted to try to get everything in that you could, before you had to go back. And there was never enough time. In the good weather, we often did something outdoors, like play baseball or fly a kite. We both loved flying kites. Actually, your love of kites reminded me of my own forgotten enjoyment. Perhaps that was true of other simple pleasures, as well. Once we went to the park, and, while you were controlling the kite, I sat down. The next thing I knew, there you were, running past me, hair flying, empty spool in hand, chasing after the kite string, which, we both learned at that moment, was not permanently attached to the reel. We managed to track down the kite and to rewind all of that string, and how we laughed!

I remember that, on my weekends with you, we used to go the video rental store on Friday to pick a movie for the evening. You always wanted a martial arts movie, usually one that was not age-appropriate. Somehow, though, we always seemed to find something satisfactory, and then we stocked up on provisions of popcorn and ice cream to accompany the night's entertainment. Our friends called the ice cream cartons "industrial size containers", but that was the kind you preferred. I still have some of those cartons. Sometimes we would go to visit friends like Don or Dale. You liked to play Ping-Pong with all of us, and you particularly loved running Don's HO train set. I have a vivid picture in my mind of you, completely absorbed in overseeing the operation of the entire layout while standing on a stepladder at the controls.

I remember the night that I told you that Mom and I were going to be divorced. You wouldn't look at me, and I asked if you were crying. You still wouldn't look at me, and I said that, if you were crying, it was OK, because I was crying. When you still wouldn't look at me, I took your hand and put it on my face, wet with tears. Only then did you turn to me, sobbing, and climb into my arms. We were crying for a future that would not be. We had no way to know what terrible things were to unfold.

And yet, I remember moments of joy and warmth in all the horror of the events of the divorce. I'll never forget the times that you expressed your feelings of frustration and anxiety -- each time, when you were done, a burden seemed to be lifted from you. I'll never forget the time you were trying to explain something to me and you said, "Dad, you understand about feelings, and so you'll understand if I tell you how I feel about this." I'll never forget how you talked on and on about school, about friends, about Cub Scouts, while we played Ping-Pong. I'll never forget how happy you were after your eighth birthday party, when we had a treasure hunt for your friends and everyone went home with a water gun. I was learning, and, I guess you were, too.

I remember that, sometimes, I had the uncomfortable feeling that I could see myself as a father through your eyes. What manner of psychological prism held me up to this sort of scrutiny? No matter. In the reflected light, I didn't always like what I saw of myself. There was no accusation of the father in the son's look, no anger, no reproach. Quite the contrary. It was business as usual. But, I didn't like it. So I felt compelled to reject the old way, to reach beyond myself to become more the father that you needed, and that I wanted you to have, and to become more the man that I wanted to be. And if the result was a gift to you, it was made possible by your loving gift to me.

And now? Now, I still have questions -- questions that may never be answered; about you, about others, about your life and your death. But, now I have memories, too.

You know, I remember how focused you could be in your play, even when you were very young. You would concentrate on what you were doing to the exclusion of all else. And then, as if reacting to some unseen stimulus, you became suddenly conscious of the world outside your own thoughts. Perhaps feeling momentarily disoriented, you would look up and, in a small, uncertain voice, you would say, "Dad, are you there?"

Yes, Andrew. I'm here. Come visit me in a dream. Anytime.

Love,
Dad

July 4, 1999

Dear Andrew,

Every man finds his demons in a different metaphoric bottle. It turns out that mine are in travel. I seem to transform every inevitable uncertainty into my own personal dread, and, without a traveling companion, I turn that dread in on myself. Sometimes, though, business and yes, curiosity, have a way of overcoming fear, at least temporarily. Later, when the deed is to be done, the optimism of the planning stage is forgotten, and I teeter on the edge of panic. I'm working on it, but right now, it's hard.

It was just such a time, a month ago, when I flew to Florida to meet a potential client about controlling railroad locomotives. As you can imagine, I, a train-lover all my life, was excited, even if terrified. What an opportunity! I actually had the chance to work professionally on trains. First, however, I had to fly to Orlando and then rent a car and drive two hours on unknown freeways. I'm not sure what happens in my head. Do I think that the road suddenly falls off the end of the earth? Still, I thought of you and your design of a locomotive that would require no fuel, and I knew that you would have been excited, too. In fact, I knew that you would have wanted me to tell them about it, in case they could make use of your idea, so I planned to do just that.

The trip down from Michigan, the night before my scheduled meeting, was tense, but manageable. I sang songs when the drive verged on endless, and, well, to get to the point, I made it. The next day passed quickly and, unfortunately, I don't think the job will work out for me (even with your idea). However, before I knew it, I was back on the road again, the seemingly interminable freeway that promised to take me back to the airport. One signpost looked like the previous, however, as I wondered with some anxiety, if the exit to the rental car facility would be well marked. In my state of agitation, I didn't know that I was comparatively well off, merely driving on a boring, over-long freeway.

Then, it hit, quite suddenly really, so that I was totally taken aback. Lightening struck all around me and rain fell so violently that I could barely see even the side of the road, much less the lane in front of me. No longer was I worried about whether the exit was well marked. Now I was worried about staying on the road, and not hitting the car in front of me!

And then I felt a presence in the car beside me -- a familiar presence. So I put my hand on the gearshift, as I had done so often years ago, and I felt a little hand on mine, resting warmly and lovingly. Was that you? And I said aloud, "Are you there, Andrew?"

With the quiet answer, I found an island of peace in this foreign vehicle on an unfamiliar road, for I knew that the raging storm existed only outside the car. Then, gradually, even the thunderstorm subsided as I completed my journey with ease.

The reply I had registered, in the midst of the turbulence, was the sweetest tone imaginable. I heard a little voice inside me say, "Yes, Dad, I'm here. I'm always here … "

And, so am I.

Love,

Dad

January 31, 2000

Dear Andrew,

So much of our lives consists of simple activities with immediate consequences that it's easy to lose ourselves in busy-ness. Turn a key and start the car. Tie the bag and take out the garbage. Open the door and leave the room. Push the button and rewind the tape. Direct actions. Purposeful actions. How about, remember the history and try to understand?

Standing on Abbey, the street where you were born and lived and where you died, I am struck by the peacefulness of things. There is nothing here that reminds me of the horrifying events that unfolded before my eyes 12 years ago. There are no visible signs of our joys and sorrows, our triumphs and frustrations, our tears and our laughter, and our final ride together. This block looks like any block in any ordinary suburban neighborhood. There are mature trees and there are lawns and driveways. Alas, driveways. No one else would know what happened here.

Now, there is only the wind, and the wind only repeats what she has heard. Who will inform the wind, if I do not? So push the button and rewind the tape. But wait. I want to tell you that this tape is ragged with playing. It has seen a lot of use, and records a lot of pain. I don't particularly relish the thought of replaying it. But, apparently, it is not yet done being played.

So, I had intended to awaken early this morning to start this letter, just to start. And this intention awakened me and made me restless at the appointed hour. I tell you that I could not face my chosen task so I hid in bed, torn with indecision. Should I get up and write what I need to write, but don't want to write, or should I stay in bed and save it for another day? I feel compelled to write this and yet afraid, but afraid of what? I'm not sure what I fear -- perhaps the pain I will rediscover, or, worse, perhaps that I lack the ability to write what I need to express, what is inside me.

That was when I clearly heard a child's footsteps echoing down the darkened hallway, and so I lay as still as I could to listen for more telltale sounds. It's funny, how much we can tell from the echo of footfalls -- how heavy, how tall. Yes, it was definite. What I heard was a child walking in the hallway, so I strained to hear confirmation. Finally, hearing no more sound, I arose to check Hannah's room. But she was fast asleep in her bed. So I ask you, was that you in the house, beckoning me to get on with it? Teasing me out of my warm bed to investigate? Was that you? Who else could it have been? But, of course, now I was up and about.

So push the button and rewind the tape. It's a simple action; but where to stop it? What year? What day? What moment? That's the question, still unanswered. I seem to have nothing but questions these days. So, I guess, push the button and rewind the tape.

Love,
Dad

March 27, 2000

Dear Andrew,

I have been trying to write the story, to put together the letters, and yet I am stymied. I sit down at the keyboard, and nothing comes -- no thought, no feeling, no words. I am mute and numb. What's going on? What don't I want to know? What am I afraid to say?

So I turn away from the page before me and announce my intention to give it up for now. And that is enough for the passion to return. It is blind and primitive, and I feel it rise slowly from depths that know no sounding. It is white hot, and it has been denied so long that, in isolation, it has fed on itself and grown turbulent. I am unprepared for the intensity of this underground river of magnum, but now I know what stays my pen. I did not want to recognize what now I see.

It is blame! I still feel so much rage inside that I don't know what to do. Your whole life was stolen from you and our lives together were cut short within a few moments, within a few heartbeats. And so I rage inside. But how can I release so much anger without aiming? So, blame just feels right; but, who to blame? Who to hold accountable for an injustice so great that it brings me to my knees?

Oh, Andrew, it is all too easy to find culprits. Big culprits and little, I can see all too clearly how they contributed to your difficulties in life and ultimately to your death.

How do I communicate all of this? How can I think when the fire of my anger burns as bright as ever? And if so, how would a letter written today differ from one written 10 years ago? And what does this say of my life?

What tender part of my soul has remained untouched and unhealed by the years? Will I ever find peace?

I miss you so much.

Love,

Dad

April 30, 2001

Dear Andrew,

As you know, I've been struggling with the circumstances of your death almost from the time it happened. What happened? Why did it happen? Who made it happen? All of these questions have swirled around in my mind, and my heart, and I have had no peace. Do I think about them everyday? No, I don't, at least not anymore. But that doesn't mean that they have gone away. Far from it. No, in some fundamental way, I have made these issues a part of myself, almost like early childhood traumas.

And, at some deep level of myself, I stand forever ready to tell the story, to tell what happened, and particularly, to tell who was to blame. That is the problem. And that is what I must write about now. For now I know that, as it was when I wrote to you long ago, so is it yet for me today. My core feelings have remained unchanged for over ten years. I still blame the same people and I'm still angry in the same way. I could make this letter about what happened, about what I feel happened, and about who I feel made it happen. But that's not what this letter is about. If it were, I would just be reliving those disturbing times up to and including your death, and, at the end, I would feel no internal change, no relief. If this letter were to be about the past, then I would stay in the past with it, and it's not the past where I want to dwell. Nor do I believe you would want me there. No, this letter is about the present. This letter is about blame itself.

It is clear to me, and yet somehow murky, but I have always known whom I could, and should, hold responsible for your death. I don't often tell my story, our story, anymore. I'm not sure why. Perhaps some, looking for signs of healing, would say that I no longer need to tell it as much because my pain and anger are no longer as raw. And perhaps that is so. But if I look inside myself honestly, the truth goes beyond this simple explanation. No, I would have to say that I still have had a strong need, as strong as ever, for people to believe what I tell them about what happened and why. And my judgment is that they do believe.

So, if that's true, why doesn't it help? Why don't I feel better, then, when I tell what happened? Why don't I feel satisfied? Why don't I begin to feel peace? Why, in fact, do I feel worse? Well, now, I'm beginning to see that I need to come to terms with my blame, and, perhaps to let it go. And that's why I'm not telling you who I blame and why. To do so, to repeat the story, would keep me stuck.

And these people that I blame, are they at fault? I can feel the energy in that question. I can feel the siren call, beckoning me back to treacherous waters. But, I'm tired. I'm weary of this particular journey that seems always to take me in circles, back to where I started. So, I return to the question. Are they at fault? Andrew, I tell you, I probably know more about what happened to you than anyone else alive, and so, if anyone could answer that question, anyone at all, it would be me. Well, Andrew, believe me. I would love to be able to answer, "Yes! They are!" But, the truth is, I honestly don't know. Deep in my heart, I just don't know. Oh, I wish I did. I have yearned to know. But I don't. And there it is, as simple and plain as I know how to be. What a relief to be able to say it. I don't know!

And yet, it is also disturbing to say it. For if they are not certainly to blame, then who is? Something so horrible, so devastating, as your death must have an explanation, mustn't it? Someone has to carry that burden of responsibility, don't they? Maybe, after all, that's the function of blame. When we imagine another shouldering a heavy load, we are inclined to forget our own. My own. I am inclined to forget my own.

What burden? What responsibility? Well, to start, as I stood watching you, as your ride into the street shifted into slow motion, I did nothing. I watched. I despaired. I hoped. I despaired again. I did not scream. I did not run. I did not move. In every other crisis in my life, when the world crawled into slow motion, I knew just what to do, and did it. But, on May 19, 1988, I did nothing. Some have suggested that what that means is that there was nothing I could do; that there was nothing that could be done. Maybe. But I will never know. How I yearn to know! But I can never know. If I had screamed, would it have changed anything? If I had run, would I have been able to get to you in time? I'll never know.

What I do know is that your death is bound up inextricably in my mind to the divorce, a divorce I wanted so that I could have enough freedom to build a good life for myself, a life with plenty of room for you and for Leah, but also with love for me. I never intended that you would not be alive to be a part of that life. And, certainly, I know that divorces do not routinely result in the death of a child. But, was it my, some would say "selfish", need that resulted in your death? If that is so, did I have a right to pursue my dream? Was I part of the cause and effect that ended in the street almost 13 years ago? I don't know. I'll never know.

What I do know is that, in spite of all my grief since your death, I have come to have a good life. It's not a trouble-free life, but a good life, filled with love and affection. I have Leah and I have a new family and they all mean the world to me, as you have. So, you see, I have grieved and I will continue to grieve, and to miss you. I will continue to wonder what you would be like as a grown man, and I will ache with the loss. But, over the years, I have risked new love and I have found new joy. If you had not died on that day, almost 13 years ago, what would my life be like now? What would it have been like for the last 13 years? Would your living somehow have excluded the possibilities and the happiness that I now take for granted? I don't know. I'll never know.

What I do know is that I am in crisis right now. I have lost my way in my career, and I have no vision for what I want or need to do. I know that I have been unhappy with my work, and I know that I am unhappy with no work. I have let go of the robot research that I conducted during your lifetime and beyond, and I have no idea what will take its place. I have many internal conflicts, and I seem to be stuck, unable to speak for myself, unable to describe myself. Worse, every time I try on a different field of endeavor, a different occupation, just to see how it will feel, I immediately lose interest in it, and then I get depressed. I have even had that happen with respect to writing, which I had felt certain, was one of my dreams. I know that I must make contact with all new people, a whole new network, and I feel paralyzed. So now, what I wonder is, what will it take? Do I deserve even the happiness I have? Do I deserve to be happy in my career? What does anyone deserve? What do I deserve? Given that you got so little from life, how can I have so much? I don't know the answers to these questions. I'll never know.

What I do know is that it's not fair to Linda or Hannah or Leah, for me to disappear into myself, for me to be less than I can be. They deserve more from me than I have been giving. Furthermore, I know that my current crisis can endanger my family's well being, because of the anxiety and concern that they must feel. So, I certainly know that I can make my good life not so good. Do I have the right to take my family down this path? I don't know.

What I now know is that I would never have found out these things about myself if I had continued on the path of blame that I initiated so many years ago. I would never have questioned, and I would never have looked into my own feelings. I would have remained stuck in unconscious guilt and my life would have stayed on hold indefinitely. At least now, I have a chance to resolve this. But, where will my new path lead? How will I get back into my life? I don't know. At least for today, I don't know.

I wish I knew. I wish …

Love, as always,

Dad

May 17, 2001

Dear Andrew,

In two more days, it will be 13 years since your death. It seems impossible, sometimes, that so much time has gone by. And lately, I have found myself, deep in thought, back on that day, with all of its horror and its imponderable questions.

I remember as if it were yesterday, that when I first saw your wagon emerge from behind the hedge and roll into the street, I knew what I was watching. As the scene played out in slow motion before me, I knew that I was about to see you die. I had one moment of hope that you might actually make it across the street, but only one. I often think that, while I was watching, I was also a participant. In my mind, I stretched those seconds before you were hit so that we could share, we could be together until the last. I hope you felt my presence.

Perhaps I don't let go of these images so that I can maintain some sense of control, but I know that control is an illusion. Perhaps I am conflicted about the good life I have, even though you are not here, but, deep down, I really don't think that you would begrudge me what I have. It's hard for me to believe that you would wish me unhappiness after all that we have meant to each other. I know now that I did my best for you when you were alive, even when it was a struggle to know what, in fact, was the best thing to do.

And so, my memory drifts to random places. A few days ago, I was in a store when I heard, on a radio somewhere, that rain was expected for the next few days. But that was OK, the announcer said, because rain was good for the flowers. And I was reminded of that day, 13 years ago, when it rained off and on, and it drizzled just after your death. And I was reminded of a song in Les Miserables by a dying girl, who doesn't feel any pain, and who concludes that " … rain will make the flowers grow". And I hope that you don't feel any pain.

And I think about keeping you safe and close, about not abandoning you, and I realize that I fought to keep you close, and I fought to keep you safe. And, once again, I realize that there is a limit to how safe anyone can keep anyone else. I can influence and, for a child, I can insist on certain choices, but they are merely the safer alternatives, not safe ones. There is no such thing as "safe", is there? This is hard for me, especially when I want, with all my heart, to protect Hannah in her youth and comparative vulnerability. Well, now I suppose that you are safe at last, and, as has been true for the last 13 years, you can finally visit me whenever you want to.

I remember that in the hours stretching to days after you died, I felt you come to me, tear-stained, terrified, asking me what had happened to you. And I could not tell you. I could not face you. I'm sorry, but I just couldn't. In some ways, it is just as hard now. Perhaps, if I focus on the time of your death, or on the chaos just before, then, in my mind, you are still alive. You are still active, still warm, still here. But, then you are still 8 years old, and still riding that wagon, over and over again. This is no way to keep you alive. You and I both deserve more.

But now, if I'm very quiet, and sit very still, I can feel you sitting in the window, behind me, watching me calmly. It is a far cry from your fear and confusion of 13 years ago. But, now I have a job to do. Perhaps it is a job that is long overdue. It is a father's job to tell his son the truth and it is a father's job to stay with his son to help him with that truth. Who helps the father? Well, I have always felt that it is the father's job to get help for himself from other adults.

And so, while you are calmly sitting, I'm going to turn around and look you in the eyes, and I'm going to say,

"Andrew, listen to me. Andrew, you died 13 years ago. Whatever happened and why it happened, none of that matters. What matters, Andrew, is that you're gone. You're really gone. And I love you and miss you."

I am always here …

Love,

Dad

May 26, 2001

Dear Andrew,

It is now one week past this year's anniversary. It has been a painful time, thinking of you. I can't help wondering what life would have like if you had lived.

You know, people do what, in their heart, they are committed to doing. If they are committed to completing a project, then they devote themselves to that project. I suppose, in reality, that people generally have multiple commitments of different priorities, so that they must divide their time between them. But, if one of them has, by far, the highest emotional pull, then that commitment dominates. It can even become impossible to engage meaningfully in anything else.

That was how it was for me before you died. I was committed to staying in your life, to being a father to you. I was committed to giving you the best life, the best emotional support that I knew how. Oh, yes. I was doing other things in my life. But, you took priority. And I could not believe then, nor can I believe now, that it would have been best for you if I had just paid child support and otherwise stayed out of your life. I also believe that that strategy would not have been good for Leah, but I must leave that discussion for another letter. This one is about you.

In fact, I felt both your need and your desire for greater contact with me, and so I fought for that. When you died, I didn't know what to do with myself. Not only did I lose you, but I also lost a major part of my reason for being. I suppose that I have written you all of these letters, in part, to continue my commitment to our relationship, because I have always known that it has been important to both of us. But the letters, as healing as they have been for me, do not take the place of our flesh-and-blood closeness.

Then, I became recommitted to the robot project that claimed my professional energy for your entire life. I know that part of the attraction of my robot research was the connection to you, and to your life. Again, as healing and exciting as it was, that work could not give me what, in life, you gave me, and that phase is over.

Yes, even in the early days of my grief for you, I was able to reach out and to love, and I am utterly committed to my relationships with Linda, Hannah and Leah, as I continue to be committed to our evolving connection.

But something is missing in my life. Sometimes, people commit themselves to negatives, such as failure, because personal success may be inconsistent with their worldview. Perhaps I am committed to something negative, but I am unaware of what that could be. No, I need to be more proactive in this.

And therefore, I am committing myself to finishing these letters to you, as a way of integrating and internalizing my love and my grief for you. This will be only the end of the first phase. No, it doesn't mean that there will be no more letters. Quite the contrary. I will continue to write to you for the rest of my life.

I know that I was afraid, for the first few years after your death, that I would forget you. As we can both see, that has not happened. I will never forget you. I will never stop loving you.

Love,
Dad

June 1, 2001

Dear Andrew,

Sometimes I am astounded when I overlook the simplest things. I don't know why I never thought of this before. All these years, it never occurred to me to calculate how fast I would have to have run to catch your wagon. Apparently, I have felt guilty about it all this time, but I never checked it out.

I have had all the information I needed since shortly after your death. So why didn't I look into it? Nothing could be simpler! I know the distance, and the police report tells how long you were in the street. They determined the time by testing the wagon, so it's a pretty reliable number. What stopped me? Was I afraid to find out? Did it just slip my mind, somehow? I don't know, but I've been ready to find out for a little while now.

So, the question is, could I have run fast enough? And the answer is that I would have to have run faster than Olympic 100 meter sprinters. And from a standing start! The true answer then, is, no, I could not have run fast enough to save you, even if I had risked death by running in front of the truck.

Now, having written this, I am relieved, and I'm sad - - sad that there was nothing I could do, perhaps then or even earlier in your life, sad that you were out of my reach, sad that my all too human limitations can have such dire consequences, and sad to see your death again, differently perhaps but with the same result. I am sad because, now, no matter how much I replay it in my mind, I can never make it right, not even if I live to be 100.

If I can't make it right, what can I do to make it better, even if just in my visualization? Is there something I could alter in my memory that would help me? The truth is, I'm weary of watching you die, over and over. It's so awful, it's beyond words.

I need to tell you something. It is something that I have only recently admitted to myself, and never to another. I am uncomfortable admitting it now, but it has been true for a long time, I think. I want you to know that there is a small part of me that is so tired of seeing you die that the prospect of death offers a kind of relief. All my grief would be, at last, at last, behind me. But, no, I don't want to die! I love life too much! I love living too much! And yet, I am afraid that this tiny, weary piece of my soul could sometime, in an unguarded moment, assume control and induce me to do something I truly do not want to do. Improbable? Yes. Impossible? I don't know, but it adds urgency to my question: what could I visualize differently?

And so I let my mind float free on the vast waters of memory, allowing myself just to drift with the currents and tumble with the swells. And then, suddenly, I am free of the surface and hovering above reality so that all things become fluid, and fact intermingles with desire.

Of course, the way I would really like to change it is so that it doesn't happen at all, but, somehow, I can't, or don't, imagine that. I see you on the wagon, but instead of focusing on the opposite side of the street, you turn your head toward me, so that we make eye contact. In my reverie, if so it is, I hear myself call out, "I need you to know that I'm there! I can do this if I know we're together!" I needed you to know that I was with you, and I needed to know that you were with me. I need to know that you are with me. Now, maybe, I can do "this", this living, if I know that you're watching, if I know that you're there.

Still in a daze from my journey within, I try to process what now stands revealed. I have never before thought in terms of needing something from my children. I wonder, is it OK to need something from you, to have needed something from you?

So, now I come back to a fundamental question that I have asked from the beginning: why did my internal clock slow down when I saw you go into the street? Why was it all in slow motion? Always before, when my world slipped into slow motion, I instinctively knew what to do, and did it. Always before, I was able to react and to minimize harm. Always before, I did all that could be done. Did my tempo turn so deliberate to tell me that I was, in fact, doing all that could be done? That has been suggested in the past, but always before, I could not believe. Now, maybe I can.

Love,
Dad

June 5, 2001

Dear Andrew,

I am so excited! We are planning a train trip across the country. This has all arisen in the last few days, and I can hardly believe that I'm going to cross the country by train yet another time.

Actually, the original plan from many months ago was that Linda and Hannah were going by themselves to Oregon to visit a dear friend. They were going to fly and I was going to stay home. Then, a combination of energies caused us to change our plans. On the one hand, Lin was beginning to urge me to go, too. Knowing that, for me, train travel offered extra incentive, she even offered to take the train instead of flying. On the other hand, I have been changing over a period of several months, and I had become excited about going west with them. But, now I was thrilled about the prospect of taking the train, especially since I had never traveled the anticipated route across the northern U.S.

So, I called Amtrak, and I was disappointed to learn that we could only book reservations for the return trip. The outbound leg was sold out on all of the reasonable travel days. Certainly, we could fly to Oregon and then take the train home, but that would not be as much fun. I took the railroad plans on as my special challenge. I have to tell you that, usually, Linda makes all the travel arrangements, but, in this case, I took over. All of a sudden, my life was invested with an energy I have rarely known, and perhaps never before at this intensity.

I have crossed the country's girth four times round trip in my life, not to mention various trips down the east coast, up the mid-heartland and innumerable voyages between Boston and Washington, DC. The train has always been like a home for me, as well as a source of adventure and camaraderie. It is a continuously moving window on the vast and wondrous world, offering scenic beauty, industrial might and glimpses of alien lifestyles, all at the same time.

I decided to try to plan a circle trip, to keep the scenery varied and fresh, and I was able to put one together quickly. It will be the trip of a lifetime. It is the stuff of dreams …

We will catch the train near our house and travel to Chicago, where we will board the California Zephyr to Denver early the next morning. There, we will disembark for three days to visit friends. At the end of that time, we will get on a different California Zephyr and continue overnight to San Francisco, where we will stop for three days to visit cousins. Then, we will take the Coast Starlight north through California to Portland, where, once again, we will get off. From there, we will take a rental car to the Oregon coast, and stay for six days. Finally, we'll return to Portland and the Empire Builder, which will carry us back to Chicago and thence, home. Whew! We'll be gone for 18 days, five of them on the train.

We'll see the Great Plains stretch off forever into the horizon. We'll see mountain ranges of all sorts -- tectonic, volcanic, and simply eroded. We'll see valleys and rivers of exotic beauty. We'll see communities in the middle of nowhere and wonder what people do there, and why they live there. We'll see sights that cannot be seen any other way. Neither Lin nor Hannah has ever traveled on such a long train trip, or even overnight. They cannot imagine the treats that await them. It will be such an adventure!

An adventure, the pure pleasure of it -- I don't think I have ever allowed myself to dream in terms of an adventure before. Certainly, I have rarely thought of such a luxury since your death. On the other hand, perhaps adventure is not a luxury after all. Perhaps my spirit needs an adventure, or a quest, for nourishment. If so, it has been starved of late. But, now, I will take my fill.

On my return, I will be sure to share with you my experiences, both on and off the train. Perhaps I should take some pictures from the window …

Love,
Dad

August 23, 2001

Dear Andrew,

Our magical train trip is over and we are home. We saw the Great Plains, the snow-covered ruggedness of the Colorado Rockies, the stark wind-swept sands of Utah and Nevada, the towering overlooks of the pine-covered Sierra Nevada, the lush greenery of the Sacramento Valley, the imperious and majestic Mount Shasta, the rock-strewn coast of Oregon, the broad canyons of Glacier National Park, and the lazy "Ole Man" Mississippi. We stayed in Denver, San Francisco and Oregon, and it was amazing. It was the first real adventure I have had in over 10 years. I have learned a lot of things about myself.

I have had the advantage of a new perspective: You see, I took this particular trip with a little, blond-haired boy, who pressed his cheek to the window even at night, so as not to miss a single moment of this fantastical journey. I saw him clearly within the dark confines of the 5-mile long Moffat Tunnel at over 10,000 feet elevation under the Continental Divide, where the train became a tunnel within a tunnel for 15 minutes. I saw his reflection in the windows looking back at me from meandering rivers and rocky gorges. And I met him surveying the spectacle of the Sierra Nevada, where rocks and Ponderosa pine trees compete for top billing. We were both mesmerized by snow-covered Mount Shasta in northern California and astounded by the vastness of the Columbia River Gorge in Washington. In his face, gazing back at me from the Mississippi River, I recognized disappointment that such a voyage need ever end, and I, well, I knew just how he felt.

For the little boy I saw was me. It was me, cavorting with antelope in Montana and it was me winding through narrow rock passes west of Winter Park, Colorado. It was me, enjoying 2,000-foot overlooks that seemed to just fall directly away from the tracks. It was me, amazed and fascinated by miles of desert that went on and on in all directions. It was me, awakening early in the morning to the sound of squealing wheels and hurrying to the lounge car to see what could cause my train to complain so mournfully. Yes, just like 53 years ago, my first transcontinental crossing by rail, it was "my" train. Just like times and trips past, I took in everything I could -- sights, sounds, sensations and friendships -- hardly daring to blink lest I miss something. So, it was me, moving back and forth, from one side of the lounge car to the other to get every perspective available. It was me, marveling at millions of years of natural craftsmanship arrayed panoramically just beyond reach on the other side of my window.

You see, to me, taking the train has always been special. It has often seemed more like flying than flying ever was. Did I say flying? I meant soaring! The train's ascension of the mountains is seemingly so effortless. All that horsepower from the three enormous passenger locomotives is far away to the fore, soundlessly leading the steady 30 mile per hour charge on uncompromising slopes, and we lucky ones, almost a quarter of a mile to the rear, just seem to float up the hill in complete defiance of gravity. The only noises to remind us that we are actually being muscled up that winding, incessant steel ribbon are the occasional "Hee … ere Coo … omes the Traa … ain" at road crossings and the expectant "Beep Beep" that announces our imminent station departures and the renewal of our adventure.

It is the train, with its particularly intimate routings through cities and towns that simply beg the question, "What is it like to live here?" After a trip like this one, it is impossible to miss that it is the railroad that first drew this nation together with its taut steel net, and still holds it firmly. The scream of the steam whistle is gone and the "clickety-clack" is all but gone, yet the constant parade of freight continues. Indeed, it is the train that reminds us of the very rhythms of life -- sometimes fast, when the road is straight and flat and there are no obstacles; sometimes tortuously slow, winding back and forth past the same perspective, with little apparent progress, until, wham, suddenly there is a long tunnel and a completely unanticipated scene on the other side; and sometimes there is no movement at all, and waiting and wanting becomes all, until another train passes and forward progress resumes.

So, it was me, the small, blond boy I used to be, coming along to tempt the adult me to come out and play. And, as you can see, play I did! And play we did! It has been a long time since I have been called out to play and I have accepted. That little blond boy has often been lost in my life. Once upon a time, another blond boy helped me to find him, by teaching me about kites and models and, well, running for the sake of running. But, after you died, he got lost again for years and years, at least until now. I have found him and I don't intend to let him get away again. He's too precious to me.

But, there's more. For it was me, learning as if for the first time, how big everything is that is associated with a railroad, whether it is locomotives or trains, mountains or cities, industries or emptiness. It is all big and I liked it. I have stretched my boundaries like never before, and they will never shrink back to their former size. How deep can any canyon seem now that I have peered over the edge of a virtually bottomless precipice? How tall can any hill appear, how impossible can any obstacle be, now that I have scaled the Rocky Mountains, foot by foot?

We arrived home late on a Monday night and immediately went to bed. Tuesday morning was sunny and I opened the front door to retrieve the newspaper from the front porch. What now confronted me was the same scene I had faced every morning since I moved into this house, 15 years ago, and yet it was not. There was something extraordinarily beautiful about the lush green trees and grass carpets before me.

It was not more verdant than the Ponderosa pine forests in the Sierra Nevada, nor more lush than the Sacramento Valley. It was not sunnier than Glacier National Park nor fresher than Evergreen, Colorado, but it was, nevertheless stunningly beautiful, more so than I have ever seen it. Hannah looked and saw it, too. What was it? After all, that view from my front door has not changed in these weeks of our absence. Perhaps, then, we are the ones who have changed. I know I have. I suppose we will never again be the same...

Love,
Dad

October 1, 2001

Dear Andrew,

I have been having horrible recurrent dreams of being hit by a car. Each dream is slightly different, but they each seem to end the same way. In each dream, I was standing or sitting by a curb at a corner -- the same corner in every dream. The street was slippery and I could see the cars skid into me, as if in slow motion.

In one dream, I was waiting on the corner (for what?) and there were several other people waiting as well. There was some music playing from somewhere and a man, a stranger, reached out to take my hand. I pulled away from him quickly -- I wanted to be left alone. Then, I thought that I would just fly away, like Superman. I tried to get off the ground, but I couldn't fly. It felt strange, as if I was used to being able to fly, and, for some reason, I couldn't this time. Oddly enough, I could go up maybe three to four feet, but no higher. Although people were looking at me and I was aware of that, I didn't worry about it. I was not self-conscious. Then, not being able to fly, I sat down on the curb. I looked up to see a car skidding toward me and onto the curb. I leaned back to avoid being hit by the bumper, but not far enough and I was hit anyway. The dream ended there and I woke up. In fact, each time the dream recurred, I awoke when I was hit, except for the last time.

In that dream, I was standing on the same street corner and I saw a car skidding toward me, as before. Everything went into slow motion, as I jumped into the air and raised my legs to avoid being hit by the front grillwork. I was successful. I landed on the hood and slid toward the windshield, as the car stopped. I must have hit my head on the glass because I became unconscious in the dream, and I could see myself, as if from above, laying half on the windshield and half on the roof of the car. I watched myself for a while, and no people appeared. Wasn't there anyone driving the car? For that matter, was anyone driving any of the cars in my dreams?

The next I knew, I was sitting next to you on a bench. It looked like one of those backless concrete benches that you see sometimes in parks in big cities. You looked the same as always -- my blonde-haired eight year old. There were so many things that I wanted to say, so many things I wanted to ask, but I couldn't find the words. So, instead of talking, I listened to you. I have to say that it was rare for you to say anything in my dreams. Now you were saying a lot.

You were telling me that it was not my time yet. No, you were not just telling me. You were leaning forward and pressing your point urgently. I still had a lot to do, you were saying. I had to be a father, for example, for Hannah and Leah, but also for others. Who? You didn't say. You stressed that I had many years left to live and you implied that it was important that I live them. And, from the way you spoke, I believe that you meant "live" in the full sense.

Then, suddenly, you were gone and the bench was gone. I was aware of being back in my body on top of the car. Apparently, I had made the choice to stay and to live. My body hurt all over, and I wondered if I would have permanent brain damage from the accident. Then, I awoke. I would sleep no more that night.

I have been somewhat shaken by the manner of contact with you and saddened as well. Now I find that, when I try to relate these overwhelming dreams to others, the feelings rise in my throat and overtake my words. I must struggle to fight for breath to express myself, and, I'm guessing, the struggle itself conveys much more than I can possibly verbalize. As traumatic as the dreams were, nevertheless, it was comforting to talk to you, and deeply reassuring. I have always experienced your visits as loving, but this one above all.

I will do as you have told me. I will try ...

Love,

Dad

December 15, 2001

Dear Andrew,

I am changed. I know that now. I knew it then, too, that my life would never be the same, but it's different somehow than it has been. Something has been happening to me lately. I'm not sure what. People have been telling me that I seem different and I know it's true. They have been saying that they can see it in my face, and I have to take their word for that. I do know lots of things that I never used to know.

I know that relationships evolve over time, and ours has been no exception. Though I always imagine you to be an eight-year-old boy, even in my dreams, I speak to you and write to you now as an adult. When did the change happen? Slowly, I imagine …

I know that, over time, pain evolves into sorrow, and sorrow, in turn, increases the capacity for joy. I know that I have much to cherish in my life, yet I know that every hello may be the last and that every goodbye is as the first.

I have climbed my mountain, foot by foot, and passed through the tunnel at the top. My emotional landscape has been varied. I have followed seemingly endless narrow canyons, winding alone in shadow, thousands of feet below the sun plain. I have traversed barren deserts until I thirsted for relief, and, at times, I have sojourned in broad green valleys, building strength for the next challenge. The final stop is not listed on this trip -- my journey is and has been my destination all along. No doubt, there will be other mountains, other canyons, other deserts, other valleys, and I will write to you about them. But, in the meantime, I have learned and I have changed.

What is the shape of things to come? It is a circle, like other circles in my life, centered in the twilight between what is felt and what is merely known, and with a diameter measured in years, not in yards. Through it all, I have found that I have learned what, deep down, I have always known. I have arrived at the place where, deep down, I have always been.

All these years, I have sought truth, hoping it would bring me peace, and I have sought peace, hoping it would help me to deal with the truth. Yet, I have been looking in all the wrong places, and while I was looking outside myself, I was unconsciously finding both within.

For the truth is well concealed in the center of all being that is in each of us. It camouflages itself by hiding in the open, where few would think to look, but I, well, I am one of the lucky ones. I have discovered it at last. It is a glimpse of play out an open window, a knowing smile at bedtime, a sleepy head resting on a shoulder, a sigh of contentment, a cheerful wave hello. It is a moment of warmth, a secret shared breathlessly, a casual glance that says nothing in particular, but says all. It is a quick impression, a flash of pride, a stolen hug, a silent tear. It is a thousand, thousand such moments, each of them a heartbeat, all of them a lifetime. It is what we were to each other. It is what we are to each other. It is all that happened. It is all that didn't.

And now? Well, I have struggled and despaired, and I have survived. I have risen and fallen, and risen again. I am changed forever, since that afternoon in May, and that's OK with me. I have held on long enough to be able to let go, and I have let go enough to find something real to hold on to.

And Andrew, this too, I know. I'm all right now ...
Love always,
Dad

Epilogue

October 22, 2010

Dear Andrew,

I said it aloud a few weeks ago. I said it in a large group, where many people heard me. I have never said it aloud before, not even to my most trusted friend. I have never said it in my deepest thoughts, not even in late night solitude, when truth stares wonderingly into the mirror of dream-glazed eyes. What have I said? I said, "I have come to a place in my life and in my grief, where I have found peace." Yes, Andrew, I have found peace. I have found peace with what I know and what I know I will never know. I am at peace with what I feel and what I do not. I am at peace with who I am and who I am not.

There, now I have written it. And now I am writing to you, that I may understand what I have said and what it means. My son, I have written you so many letters over the years -- letters full of discord, full of questing, full of pain. Now, this letter is different because I am different -- even more different than at the time of my last letter. I don't know how visible these differences are to others because people are such subtle reflecting glasses.

In any case, I'm on new ground, writing to you about this. I don't know if I know how to write about peace. How do I write about the absence of turmoil, the absence of anguish? How do I write about the absence of pain and anger so close to the surface that they suffused my life for so long?

Oh, I'm still sad, sad for you, sad for all my losses, but especially yours. Yet that sorrow has gone deep within me, and like a liquid, it has found its level in every cell and every pore, flowing simultaneously to every extremity and to my core, so that it is an integral part of me.

In retrospect, back at the beginning, I read poetry about being patient with sadness, but, while it resonated in my brain, I never fully understood it until now. My future was written in my grief and pain and I needed time to read and comprehend it. I needed to know the truths of life and being, and to internalize them. Perhaps one of those truths is about peace.

For so much of my life, even that now distant part before your death, I thought that peace, true peace, was an absence of discord, an end to troubling thoughts, a space where my mind would no longer drive me crazy. I wondered if I could ever find peace in my life. I wondered if serenity would forever elude me.

After you died, and for a long time, I stopped thinking about finding peace. After what happened to you, I knew, deep in my heart that peace would never be attainable. Instead, I suppose, I tried, one day at a time, merely to accept whatever I felt, whatever I thought. And so, I confess, it was with no small surprise that I heard myself say aloud, before people I mostly had never met, that I have found peace. And there it is again, that phrase that seems so pregnant with meaning. But, what meaning?

I can certainly tell you what this feeling of peace is not. It is not an end to worry, to fear, to anger. I am still, after all, a human being. But I no longer struggle with these so-called negative expressions of self. I no longer fight against these natural by-products of caring, about myself and others, and I no longer subject myself to self judgment on the basis of my internal make-up.

But what is it, this peace? I can tell you what now I know. I know that I have been mistaken about peace all along. I know that peace like this is no mere absence. It is not a void, a vacuum in the place inside me where intense energy once defined my very being. It is not like outer space, whose tranquility is merely a lifeless emptiness. If my peace were such a pressureless void, nature would find a way to fill it. Ideas, thoughts, feelings would come tumbling in, haphazard and tumultuous, and any initial perception of accord would quickly drown in a deluge of random vortices -- a tortuous plasma of conflicting white hot feelings.

No, this peace is definitely a presence, not an absence. It is an acceptance, a form of being. It is the living presence seemingly of another species. It is the organic extension of another dimension. It is timeless and yet of the moment. It is more than the tranquility of the ocean depths, for that is but the inertia of water's weight, ponderous and insensible. This peace is solemn, yes, but sensible and even sensitive. It does not seek to crush, but to reach out, to share by harmonizing all that it touches. It is a soft melody that sings in the beating of the heart, soundlessly, hoping that all can hear. This peace is the soul of passion and compassion. It knows death and yearns for life. It comprehends and respects age and it embraces youthfulness, without need of youth. It is a positive pressure that exactly balances within against without, above against below, open against closed. It is the soft voice of experience, and even wisdom, and it is no longer silent.

It says, "Come to me with your woes and I will share my caring. Come to me with your sorrow and I will share my understanding. Come to me with your despair and I will share my hope."

And I hope that you, too, have found peace, my son.

Love,

Dad

ABOUT THE AUTHOR

Robert Goor is a husband, a father, a writer, a mathematician and a scientist. He has been writing for over 20 years and has been a father for over 40. Dear Andrew is his first literary publication. He is an active member of the Bethesda Writer's Center and of The Compassionate Friends.

ABOUT THE ARTIST

Robin Calzadillas is an artist and illustrator living in New York City, where she designs book and album covers, tattoos, and original paintings, and is in process of developing a graphic novel.

Made in the USA
Middletown, DE
30 September 2016